ABRAHAM LINCOLN

*A BIOGRAPHIC TRILOGY
IN SONNET SEQUENCE*

By

DELLA CROWDER MILLER

Edited By
ORVILLE CROWDER MILLER

Volume One

ABRAHAM LINCOLN: THE BOY

(*Annotated* and *Illustrated*)

THE CHRISTOPHER PUBLISHING HOUSE
BOSTON, U.S.A.

ABRAHAM LINCOLN

A Biographic Trilogy in Sonnet Sequence

Volume One

COPYRIGHT © 1965
By
DELLA CROWDER MILLER
(All Rights Reserved)

Library of Congress Catalog Card Number 64-22912

PRINTED IN
THE UNITED STATES OF AMERICA

THIS LINCOLN TRILOGY

IS DEDICATED

TO

MY SON

ORVILLE CROWDER MILLER

who is also
MY LITERARY PAL

GENERAL PREFACE TO THIS TRILOGY

ABRAHAM LINCOLN
1809-1865

To pen the Lincoln story is to write
An epic of America anew,
For indissolubly their struggles grew.
The Lincoln climb was long and hard; his light
Held high, reflected honor, justice, might
That paralleled our young Republic's view.
He held its cause for freedom, dared construe
Man's rights, dared say: "Enslavement is a blight."

"A house divided cannot stand," he cried,
While greed and hate bred war and mutiny;
And then he prayed, while all the air flamed red.
He prayed for LOVE—then came the turn of tide:
A race franchised, a saved Democracy.
But in that hour of triumph, he—lay dead!

ACKNOWLEDGEMENTS

One of our Lincoln authors, Ida M. Tarbell, has said: "When your interest in Lincoln is known, people press to aid you." That this statement is true has been proven during the writing of this Lincoln biography. Educators, Lincoln authors, critics on poetic form and many friends have offered willing service, each in his own way. To all of these I extend my sincere thanks. Space permits special mention of but a few.

For the scholarly counsel and helpfulness of the late Dr. Marion Dolores Pratt, I am indeed fortunate and grateful. She was one of the editors of *The Collected Works of Abraham Lincoln,* 8 volumes, put out by the Abraham Lincoln Association. Because of this, her experience with leading Lincoln authors, and her necessary wide research in Lincoln literature, she came to be regarded as one of our best informed and most reliable Lincoln scholars. After the death of her husband, Dr. Harry E. Pratt, she was appointed by Governor William G. Stratton, to fill out her husband's term of office as Illinois State Historian.

Dr. Marion Dolores Pratt read the three volumes of this Lincoln biography as they were produced, and marveled that all essentials of the story of Lincoln's life are included here in this brief Trilogy. She then offered encouraging and safeguarding comments on each volume, often pointing out helpful source material by naming author, book and page without a moment's hesitation to recall. Few others could have offered a more thoroughly appreciated or acceptable service.

Also to the memory of Dr. Benjamin P. Thomas, I am truly grateful. But nine days before his untimely death, he read two of the manuscripts of this Lincoln Trilogy and wrote his commending comments.

I am deeply grateful to Dr. Allan Nevins, formerly of the history faculty, Columbia University, New York City, and now with Huntington Library, San Marino, California. The author of two volumes on Lincoln and others on historical subjects, he won the Pulitzer Prize for Biography in both 1933 and 1937. Dr. Nevins' comprehensive and encouraging comments came early in the development of this Lincoln biography and proved to be a spur throughout its writing, especially when research seemed endless and often vain, and health and courage sagged.

To Dr. Herman B. Wells, Chancellor of Indiana University, Bloomington, go my thanks for a like commendation of "the pains the author has taken to proof her statements" in this Lincoln Trilogy.

I thank Dr. Charles H. Coleman, Eastern Illinois University, Charleston, for his helpful "Abraham Lincoln and Coles County: A Chronology," letters, and articles on the immediate ancestors of Abraham Lincoln: Thomas Lincoln and his wife Sarah Bush Lincoln and their families. Dr. Coleman has written and published many

Acknowledgements

articles, but I am especially indebted to his *Lincoln's Lincoln Grandmother,* recently reprinted in book form.

For other encouraging helpfulness and comments, I extend gratitude to Dr. Paul L. McKay, president of Millikin University, to Dr. Alton O. Kaul, pastor of Westminster Presbyterian Church, to Dr. W. W. Cutlip, pastor of First Methodist Church, and to Dr. Carrel W. Flewelling, builder and former pastor of Central Christian Church, all of Decatur, Illinois; and to the Reverend Paul Martin, pastor of First Presbyterian Church, Holt, Michigan, and to Dr. Donald W. Miller, president of Curry College, Milton, Massachusetts.

To the Reverend Charles A. Anderson, national secretary of the Presbyterian Historical Society, Philadelphia, Pennsylvania, I express appreciation for his favorable comments upon this poetic biography.

To Dr. Louis A. Warren, director of the Lincoln Life Foundation, Fort Wayne, Indiana, and author of widely used Lincoln books and articles, go my sincere thanks for his endorsement of the care that I have taken to document my statements dealing with controversial subjects, by citing my authenticating source in Addenda Notes.

To the courteous, helpful spirit of Otto R. Kyle, former editor of the *Decatur Review* editorial page, and author of the recent book, *Abraham Lincoln in Decatur,* go my sincere thanks. When Mr. Kyle learned that I was planning to write a Lincoln biography, he immediately brought to my home sixteen of his most reliable Lincoln books and placed them on my shelves for me to use. He has read my entire three manuscripts and has contributed helpful research and editorial comment.

I also thank Mrs. J. R. Fitzgerald for a similar courtesy. She brought to me the four volumes of Ida M. Tarbell's *Life of Lincoln,* and left them with me to use.

To critics and authorities on poetic form, from whom I sought and received criticisms and suggestions without which I scarcely could have succeeded with this briefer Lincoln biography, I am deeply indebted and grateful. For, to reduce required reading time to a minimum, I chose a *sonnet sequence* poetic form in which to tell, with briefest possible wordage, the full story of Lincoln's life, deleting none of its essential elements. And, to assure that I correctly observed each detail required by this sonnet form, and that its use was appropriate for handling biographic subject matter for which the sonnet had never before been used in sequence, each of several outstanding critics of poetic form read one or more of the three volumes in manuscript form, made a critical analysis of each sonnet, and offered approval or proposed corrections of each.

The outcome is a critically-approved-and-achieved successful use of this compact poetic form, the sonnet as a stanza in a poetic continuity, to so reduce wordage, and likewise reading time, that this entire Trilogy can be read in approximately three hours of each of three evenings, as tests of average readers have proven. I shall forever be thankful to all who have helped in any way, but my deepest gratitude I here bestow upon these authorita-

Acknowledgements xiii

tive critics of poetic form for their many, many hours of devoted and invaluable assistance.

Dr. Van Chandler, author of four books and Poet Laureate of Texas, read two of these biographic sonnet sequence manuscripts, carefully analyzed each sonnet's substance and form, and gave encouraging approval.

Clarence O. and Marie L. Adams, he president of the American Poetry League, and she, with him, co-editor of that association's quarterly periodical and annual anthology, read this entire biography and made critical analysis of each sonnet. At one time they reported finding similarities to Milton, in the arrangement of subject matter, and at a later date they likened the rhythmic movement of the sonnets of this Trilogy to the easy-flowing cadence of Elizabeth Barrett Browning's *Sonnets from the Portuguese.*

To the memory and continuing inspiration of two of our most scholarly poetry critics, I owe much of any poetic values to be found in this Trilogy. I refer to Mary O'Connor, past president of the American Poetry League, author and pen artist, and originator and Chairman of World Poetry Day; and to my former—and continuing —teacher, Dr. Clement Wood, an authoritative international poetry critic who wrote twenty books, two of which I name as the best attainable on poetic forms today: *Poet's Handbook,* and *Wood's Rhyming Dictionary.*

William Sharp, of Scotland, through his most commendable book, *Sonnets of this Century,* cited to me first by Dr. Wood, has aided me materially, particularly in his treatment of the history of the sonnet, its rules and development.

Margery Swett Mansfield, Morrisville, Vermont, through her book, *Workers in Fire,* and through her elucidation of the various sonnet forms as she explained them to me by correspondence, was most illuminatingly helpful. She impressed upon me again the urgency of knowing not only the form of the Petrarchan sonnet, but also the need to study each sonneteer's sonnets to discover how differently accented languages, and the law of natural scansion, had changed the Petrarchan original form.

To Gail Brook Burket go my thanks for her helpful encouragement at the beginning of this biography.

For other indispensable services, I express sincere appreciation to the librarians of the several libraries which have furnished books of source material, including the Library of Congress, Washington, D.C.; the Illinois State Historical Library and the Illinois State Library in Springfield; the Lincoln Room of the Library of the University of Illinois in Champaign; and the Decatur Library and library of the *Herald-Review* of Decatur, Illinois. But for the services of these gracious librarians this Trilogy could not have been completed.

For the skillful services of Pearl E. Brown, who assisted with the arrangement of the indices of the three manuscripts, I am indeed thankful.

I am deeply grateful to my daughter-in-law, Dorothy Munns Miller, for her meticulous gathering and recording of data for the special card-catalogue which the Editor of this Lincoln Trilogy used in compiling its Bibliography and Illustrations and Maps sections in collaboration with my own research.

Perhaps to no one person, however, do I owe more than to my son, Orville Crowder Miller, author, editor, university professor, and minister of the gospel, whose warm-hearted sympathy and understanding, wise counsel and keen criticism, and helpful editing have consistently safeguarded me throughout the nine years of the writing of this biography of Abraham Lincoln.

To Congressman William L. Springer I gratefully acknowledge the welcome assurance of the following, which is received from him as these manuscripts go to the publisher:

"I have read many books on Lincoln but none have given greater historical significance than has your biographical trilogy, which struck me with terrific impact! It seems that I was not just reading the story of Lincoln, but was transported back to his time and was by his side as he lived life."

INTRODUCTION

When one learns of a new biography of Abraham Lincoln he may wonder what more can be said than has been said in the 6,000 monographs, stories, poems, plays, articles and biographies that are reported to have been published about this great man.

But more should and will be written, for much that has been thought to be known is still controversial or inconclusive, requiring further research and report; and, besides, new ways are needed to reach those who have not yet been enabled to read the Lincoln story as we do know it.

Findings of the Abraham Lincoln Association, organized in 1909 in Springfield, Illinois, have made an important contribution to Lincolniana, especially in two of its major releases: *The Day-by-Day Activities of Abraham Lincoln,* 4 volumes, and *The Collected Works of Abraham Lincoln,* 8 volumes. These monumental works, in addition to the release of the Lincoln private papers that had been placed by Robert Todd Lincoln in the Library of Congress to be opened in 1947, have shed much new light on controversial statements, and have served to clarify many others and motivate additional works on Lincoln.

Although the author of this biography has retold the Lincoln story, she has added some new material which she has applied largely to the illuminating and elucidating of local and national conditions that were prevalent in Lincoln's day. She has also included footnotes and addenda notes with documentation of controversial statements, and has provided helpful maps and photographic illustrations, to authenticate and vivify her presentation. But, primarily, she has given the Lincoln story an entirely new treatment through the use of an especially adapted and appropriate literary form.

While this biography is *intended for the general reader,* it is especially written for those *whose reading time is limited.* During the author's twelve years of teaching in American universities, she came to realize the welcome influence of the Lincoln life as a character builder on the student. This led her to regret the lack of a more condensed, yet complete, portrait of Lincoln, for such a biography would permit those who are limited for cultural reading time the privilege of reading it. The author's chief aim in writing this biography, therefore, has been to try to meet this need.

For the past quarter century, several Lincoln authors have attempted to write a full, yet shorter, biography of Lincoln, based upon the Abraham Lincoln Association findings. One of the most recent—a biography that has been regarded as one of the best yet produced—is written in the choicest of English prose, and not a word could be deleted from it, yet five or six evenings of from three to four hours each are required to read it! As this author laid that book aside she doubted that a more concise, and yet complete, biography of Lincoln could be written *in prose*.

Then came the challenge: *"Why not a Lincoln biography in poetry?"* She had published both prose and poetry and was well aware of the economy of words in poetry—that the poet can state in a few sentences what would require a page for the prose writer, with his many unnecessary words in his more repetitious and detailed account. And, besides, she realized that poetry was a form which Lincoln himself enjoyed. He not only wrote verse, loved, read and quoted poetry, but often carried in his pocket one of Shakespeare's poetic plays to rest and relax him in his moments of leisure.

She knew that such a venture would be a tremendous and daring undertaking, yet within a few months she had begun her research through Lincoln sources for his life story, and through American histories for her development of the national background. Soon she had also searched through various textbooks of poetry for a suitable poetic form, giving consideration to, among others: the lyric, free verse, blank verse, and the formal and informal sonnet when used as a stanza in a sequence. After thorough deliberation and trial, she decided upon the sonnet since it best met the needs of a biography or continuity of the magnitude of one dealing with Lincoln.

One of the basic influences which led this author to use the sonnet was that it is the highest form of literature.

Since her biography was to convey to the reading public the life story of one of the world's most eminent men, the sonnet seemed altogether appropriate. Moreover, though many laudable poems have been written of Lincoln, and at least one book of commendable poetry about him was released almost fifty years ago by its author, Denton Jaques Snider, the Italian sonnet form, either alone or in sequence, seems not to have been used in any of these.

In addition to shortening the wordage of the biography by use of the sonnet sequence, this author has divided the Lincoln story into three distinct periods of Lincoln's life. This she felt would be a further convenience to the reader, and an orderly arrangement for his recalling of any special details. These three partitions she has entitled, *Abraham Lincoln: The Boy, Abraham Lincoln: The Man,* and *Abraham Lincoln: The President.* Each constitutes a separate volume, and the three are now published as *A Lincoln Trilogy.* Any volume of these three *can* be read without reference to the others, and *each can be read in one evening* of from three to four hours, by the average reader, as has been proven by tests.

Volume I lists and traces the Lincoln-Hanks ancestors from England through Eastern and Southern states into Kentucky, where Abraham Lincoln was born and spent almost the first eight years of his life before he migrated with his family into the "free territory" of Indiana. Here, all through his youth, he revealed, for one of his age, a most unusually keen interest in all about him, including the well-being of all men; and, even during this early period of his life, he wrote and spoke in behalf of national interests. At the age of twenty-one, he moved with his family to Decatur, Illinois. The following year he left his father's home and sought life "on his own."

Volume II mirrors the struggling youth merging into manhood, tempered by hardships, trials, disappointments and defeat. It features his legal work, his State Assembly and National Congressional work, his marriage, the birth of his four sons, his circuit travels and his debates with Stephen A. Douglas, and at the age of fifty-two his being nominated and elected President of the United States.

Volume III depicts Lincoln as the President of a nation torn by dissention and strife, by hate and war and by bloodshed and heartache; yet it reveals how Lincoln proved himself to be a just and able leader whose mental and spiritual development had prepared him to be "the one man of the hour" for the preservation of this American Republic, and for the re-uniting of its people under one government and one flag.

Since this is said to be *the first Lincoln biography written in sonnet sequence,* it may be helpful to the reader to trace, briefly, the rise and development of the sonnet into the highest form of literature. It had its origin in Italy where the word *sonnet* meant a "little song." It consisted of a single theme running throughout its fourteen, largely but not exclusively, iambic pentameter lines, rhymed as follows through its first eight lines, or octave: *abba, abba,* and permitting only two rhymes. This was followed by the chorus, or sestet, consisting of six lines, rhyming *cdecde* or *cdcdcd,* which rhymes must be different from those of the octave.

This *informal* "little song" had been composed and sung for many years in Italy, when about the middle of the 13th century, Francesco Petrarca or *Petrarch,* then Crown Poet of Italy, made this informal song into *a formal poem.* His precedence soon prescribed many so-called "fixed rules," not only for the sonnet's form, but for its subject matter as well, such as: "Introduce the subject in the first quatrain, emphasize it in the second quatrain, and re-emphasize it in the sestet and close it with a climax." It was also thus prescribed that every line should have a full stop, which in time became known as "end-stop lines."

As *this sonnet-poem* form *spread* over Italy and into the other countries, France, Spain, Portugal, England and elsewhere, many of the poets refused to observe Petrarch's major rulings, such as the prescribed distribution of subject matter, and the "end-stop lines." Yet most of these poets adhered to the other rulings, especially those concerning the octave, the first eight lines. Today, after six centuries, we find the octave but little changed from the way Petrarch left it—with the same *predominantly* iambic pentameter lines, with a different metric foot substituted occasionally to meet the demands of the law of natural scansion.

But not so with the sestet. It has been submitted to many experimentations, consisting of changes largely in the *minor* rulings. Very often these rulings were consciously or unconsciously changed, largely because of the various languages being inflected differently, and also as a reflection of the characteristics of the people where the sonneteer lived. We find such reflections in the sonnets of Spain, Portugal, and even parts of Italy and France. Their sonnets have a freer, easier-flowing *informal lilt* that reflects the happy, easy-going manner of the thinking and living of these peninsular peoples. Such cadence is not often found in the sonnets of other countries.

In England, the different sonnet forms reflect more the *preference* of the various sonneteers, such as that which we find demonstrated by Shakespeare, Milton, Wordsworth and others. These authors refused the "end-stop lines" and some, the Petrarchan arrangement of subject matter.

Shakespeare united octave and sestet into "a fourteen line poem." His arrangement consisted of three quatrains with the privilege of from four to six rhymes, rhymed every other line and with a different rhyming couplet at the end. Because of this freedom of many rhymes, it is one of the easiest forms known.

Milton and Shakespeare agreed in the uniting of octave and sestet, but disagreed in the arrangement of subject matter. Milton preferred that the thought progress from idea to idea and line to line, instead of re-emphasizing the thought form from quatrain to quatrain. Nor did Milton employ the Shakespearean rhyming couplet at the end of the initial twelve lines. But while Milton was lauded by the critics as a poet whose sonnets became "a trumpet," the sonneteers and populace preferred the easier Shakespearean form, with its many allowable rhymes and its freer revision. And so today, the two most preferred forms are *the Shakespearean* and the revised freer form of *the Petrarchan*. While they are radically different in form, who can say that one is better than the other? The choice remains a matter of use with the author, and of taste with the reader.

This Lincoln sonnet sequence is Petrarchan in its major fundamentals such as length of line, *predominantly* iambic meter, and the separation of octave and sestet, all of which Petrarch adopted from the *informal* "little song." But this present writer's arrangement of subject matter and end-stops is influenced strongly by the Miltonic treatment, in that the unfoldment of the Lincoln story flows in natural story-sequence, rather than by the reiteration of thought form from quatrain to quatrain. And these Lincoln sonnets are *predominantly informal,* in that the author adheres to the informal setup of the original "little Italian song" in her general use of *the sonnet as a stanza in sequence.* By this informal procedure, she avoids the monotony of a too-frequent repetition of the emphases in the formal, such as the arrestive statement at the beginning of each sonnet and the decided climax at the end of every fourteen lines, which in time would reduce any story to a sing-song *do-re-mi* monotony.

In adhering to the informal elements of "the little song," she likewise deletes some of the Petrarchan minor rulings for *the higher law of naturalness,* such as is required for all natural speech and writing, *the law of natural scansion.*

The reader may find, however, many *formal sonnets in this Sequence,* placed usually at the opening of some new phase of the story, or in closing it, or occasionally as a lone sonnet used to re-emphasize some element of the story.

Now, we have seen that there are almost as *many varieties of the sonnet* as there are recognized sonneteers. But we should also further clarify for the reader that the fundamentals which distinguish the sonnet, as such, remain the same regardless of small deletions from or additions to the rulings. To illustrate: the "Peace Rose" was basically a white rose which the florist pollinated with the pollen of the yellow and pink rose and thus glorified with these colors, but in *no* way has this process *changed* its *classification* as a rose. Again, let us use the five races of man, who differ in color and custom, but are unchanged in the fundamental distinguishing elements that classify them each as Mammalia or man. So it is with the sonnet. There are many varieties, but there are only two distinctly preferred sonnet forms today.

Of the several *national and international critics* who have read these Lincoln manuscripts, one has written: "These sonnets are Petrarchan-Italian in fundamentals, but they are strongly Miltonic in thought treatment, and like Milton's they sound a trumpet that stirs the soul." Another wrote: "While these Lincoln sonnets are Italian in form, they possess the charm and easy-flowing lilt of the sonnets of Elizabeth Barrett Browning, and they are equally as effective."

Perhaps, *one of the most comprehensive comments* that has come to the author's desk was written by Dr. Allan Nevins, author of two Lincoln volumes and several other books of American history, and twice winner of the Pulitzer Prize for Biography. Dr. Nevins, now of Huntington Library, San Marino, California, and formerly of the history department, Columbia University, New York City, states in a letter to the author of this Trilogy:

"As history your statements are accurate, in places penetrating, full of fine feeling and altogether worthy of the theme. You have chosen the most difficult form of verse and have acquitted yourself well. The poetry is fluent, polished and most interesting.

"I do heartily approve of your historic and biographic treatment. You have placed your Lincoln against the background of the development of state and nation, and have accomplished this in a way beyond the reach of any prose writer...

> *"I fully realize what long years of toil have gone into these books, and I, like others, feel a deep gratitude to you for what you have done. Your perseverance in your great task, your devotion to a high aim, will in time, be valued by thousands in a fitting way."*

And now, after spending nine years in the preparation of these Lincoln books, nine of the most strenuous and yet happiest and most beneficial years of the author's life, she releases this Lincoln Trilogy with a feeling of humbleness in that the achieved ends are far removed from the visualized ideals. It is her wish, however, that the reader, in turning these pages in his walk with Abraham Lincoln, may find the reading as pleasurable and beneficial to him as the writing has been to the author.

D. C. M.

ABRAHAM LINCOLN

A Biographic Trilogy in Sonnet Sequence

Volume One

ABRAHAM LINCOLN: THE BOY

PREFACE TO VOLUME ONE

THE PIONEER LINCOLN BOY
1809-1831

The wildwood days of Lincoln's early life,
His intellect that viewed life as a whole,
His kindly heart, his consecrated soul
Beguile the reader's sympathies. His strife
As pioneer, his craving knowledge—rife
Throughout his time—with too few schools his dole,
His reaching up alone to gain the goal
God meant, thrill all of us, like martial fife!

We marvel at his leadership and see,
Despite the critics of his day, the hand
Divine that led him on to victory.
We search his ancestors, for native brand
Of blood from which such fiber came to be,
To find both blood and faith had made him stand.

SIX ASCENDING GENERATIONS OF LINCOLN-HANKS

I

SAMUEL LINCOLN of Hingham, England	THOMAS HANKS of Malmesbury, England
Came to Massachusetts in 1637	Came to Virginia before 1653
Born - 1619 Died - 1690	Born - 1630 (?) Died - 1676 (?)

II

MORDECAI LINCOLN, SR.	WILLIAM HANKS, SR.
Born - 1657 Died - 1727	Born - 1650 (?) Died - 1704

III

MORDECAI LINCOLN, JR.	JOHN HANKS
Born - 1686 Died - 1736	Born - 1690 (?) Died - 1740

IV

JOHN LINCOLN	JOSEPH HANKS
Born - 1716 Died - 1788	Born - 1725 Died - 1793

V

CAPTAIN ABRAHAM LINCOLN	LUCY HANKS
Born - 1744 Died - 1786	Born - 1766 Died - 1825

VI

THOMAS LINCOLN	NANCY HANKS
Born - 1778 Died - 1851	Born - 1783 Died - 1818

VII

ABRAHAM LINCOLN

Born - 1809   Died - 1865

FIVE DESCENDING GENERATIONS OF LINCOLN

VII

Married

ABRAHAM LINCOLN		MARY TODD	
Born - Feb. 12, 1809		Born - 1818	
Died - Apr. 15, 1865	56 years	Died - 1882	64 years

VIII
Children

ROBERT TODD LINCOLN
Born - 1843
Died - 1926   83 years
EDWARD BAKER LINCOLN
Born - 1846
Died - 1850   4 years

WILLIAM WALLACE LINCOLN
Born - 1851
Died - 1862   11 years
THOMAS TODD LINCOLN
(TAD)
Born - 1853
Died - 1871   18 years

IX
Married

ROBERT TODD LINCOLN
Born - 1843
Died - 1926   83 years

MARY HARLAND
Born - 1846
Died - 1937   91 years

X
Children

JESSIE LINCOLN
Born - 1875
Died - 1948   73 years
Married Warren Beckwith
Two children, Mary and Robert

ABRAHAM A. LINCOLN
Born - 1873
Died - 1890   17 years
No descendants.
The last of the Lincoln name.
MARY LINCOLN
Born - 1869
Died - 1938   69 years
Married Charles Isham
3014 North Street
Washington, D. C.   1 child.

XI

MARY LINCOLN BECKWITH
Born - 1898
Unmarried, lives at
2908 North Street
Washington, D. C.
ROBERT LINCOLN BECKWITH
Born - 1904
Married Mrs. Hazel Holland Wilson
6315 Ridgewood Avenue
Chevy Chase, Maryland. No blood heirs.

LINCOLN ISHAM
Born - 1892
Married Leaholma Correa
Drake Hotel
New York City.   No children

CONTENTS

Abraham Lincoln: General Preface to this Lincoln Trilogy	vii
ACKNOWLEDGEMENTS	ix
GENERAL INTRODUCTION to this Lincoln Trilogy	xvii
The Pioneer Lincoln Boy: Preface to Volume One of Trilogy	3
Six Ascending Generations of Lincoln-Hanks; Five Descending Generations of Lincolns: A Guide Chart	5

LINCOLN HERITAGE OF ABRAHAM LINCOLN

Genealogy	17
Britain's Loss, 1633	18
The First Lincolns in America, 1633	19
Sam Lincoln in Massachusetts, 1637-1690	20
The Lincoln Clan, 1637-1865	21
Mordecai, Son of Samuel, 1657-1727	22
The Broken Family	23
Mordecai Jr. in New Jersey	24
Mordecai Jr.'s Two Wives	25
Mordecai Jr. Moves to Pennsylvania	26
England's Unjust Tax, 1773	27
Tea in Pappy's Shoes, 1773	28
The Lincolns and the Boones	29
Shenandoah Virginia, 1768	30
Industrial Independence	31

War! War! War! 1775 32
"Virginia John," 1778 33
The Lincoln Gift 34
Abraham Woos Bathsheba 35
Abraham Commissioned Captain 36
Kentucky, 1784 37
Lincoln Buys Kentucky Land 38
Captain Lincoln, 1784 39
Revenge, May, 1786 40
Rescue 41
Bereavement 42
"Cousin Hananiah Lincoln" 43
Hananiah Tells About the War, September 11, 1777 44
France Recognizes America, 1777 45
Bathsheba Lincoln 46

HANKS HERITAGE OF ABRAHAM LINCOLN

Thomas Hanks, An English Prisoner, 1643 49
Thomas Hanks, 1644-1676 50
William Hanks 51
John and Joseph Hanks 52
Joseph Moves to Kentucky, 1782-1784 53
Accusers 54
Some Hanks History, 1790-1796 55
Thomas and Elizabeth Sparrow 56
Tom Lincoln Learns a Trade 57
Tom and Nancy Fall in Love 58
The Wedding, June 12, 1806 59

Tom Lincoln, An Apprentice, 1806-1808	60
Anticipation	61
Tom Buys Another Farm	62
On Nolin Creek, 1808	63
Christmas Eve in Nolin Creek Cabin, 1808	64
Visualizing Joy, February 11, 1809	65
A Blustery Winter Night, February 11, 1809	66

BOYHOOD AND YOUTH OF ABRAHAM LINCOLN

A Son Is Born, February 12, 1809	69
His Name Is Abraham	70
Babyhood	71
The Lien on Tom's Land	72
"I Must Collect!"	73
The Move to Knob Creek	74
Abe Goes to School	75
The Lincolns Go to Church	76
Playmates	77
Abe Learns the Forest Language	78
Life on the Pike	79
Clash of Class	80
The Forced Decision, 1816	81
The Move to Indiana Begun	82
The Basket Dinner	83
Tom and Nancy Visit in "E-town"	84
Tom's Last Visit with His Mother, Autumn, 1816	85
The Lincolns Leave Kentucky	86
Enroute to Indiana, Autumn, 1816	87

The Half-Face Camp, Autumn, 1816	88
Abe Learns to Use the Axe	89
The Lincolns Find Food	90
Pioneer Courage	91
The Home Was Church and School	92
The Memory Test	93
Tom Continues His Story	94
The Burial of Captain Lincoln	95
Character Building	96
Abe and Master Crawford, 1818-1819	97
A Church Is Built	98
The New Cabin, 1817	99
The Lincoln Library	100
The Letter	101
Reunion	102
The Milk-Sick Scourge, 1818	103
Madonna of the Wildwood, October 5, 1818	104
Nancy's Burial	105
"Saint John of the Wilderness"	106
Longings and Memories	107
Tom Sees a Need	108
Absence	109
Lonesome Children	110
The Big Wagon, December, 1819	111
The Stepmother	112
Intellectual Awakening	113
The Lincoln Creed	114
Abe's School at Fourteen, 1823	115

Table of Contents

Abe Begins to Write and Speak, 1821-1825	116
His Last School, 1826	117
Abe Reads The Indiana Statutes	118
The Pioneer's Son	119
Abe the Hired Man and Clerk	120
Abe Earns His First Dollar, 1828	121
Abe Goes to New Orleans, 1828	122
Sarah Lincoln Grigsby's Death, January, 1828	123
An Annual Tragedy, 1828	124
The Coffin-Maker	125
The Milk Sickness Again, 1829	126
Planning to Move to Illinois, 1829-1830	127
The Journey Begun, February, 1830	128
They Cross the Wabash	129
Illinois	130
The Prairies of Illinois	131
An Incident	132
Spring Rains	133
The Arrival at Decatur, March, 1830	134
The Welcome, March, 1830	135
Foreshadowings	136
The Visit	137
The Sangamon Cabin	138
Tom Skilled in Carpentry	139
Breaking the Prairie Sod	140
The Housewarming	141
Abe's Girl Friends	142
The Quadrille	143

Self-Analysis	144
Abe Wins Fame as a Rail-Splitter	145
Abe's First Political Speech, Decatur, 1830	146
At Autumn's Dawn	147
The Deep Snow, December-March, 1830-1831	148
The Nine-Weeks' Blizzard, 1830-1831	149
The Sheriff's Guest, January, 1831	150
The Melting Snows and Floods, February, 1831	151
March Came	152
Tom's Farewell	153
ADDENDA NOTES	155
BIBLIOGRAPHY	177
INDEX	201

LIST OF ILLUSTRATIONS

Abraham Lincoln—Pioneer Youth	14a
The Parish Church at Hingham, Norfolk, England	14b
"The Old Ship" Church in Hingham, Massachusetts	14b
Little Mound Meeting House, Hodgenville, Ky.	14b
Pigeon Creek Church, in Spencer Co., Indiana	14b
House of Mordecai Lincoln, at Scituate, Mass.	14c
House of Mordecai Lincoln, Jr., in Exeter, Pa.	14c
House of Jacob Lincoln, Shenandoah Valley, Va.	14c
Hughes Station, Floyd's Creek, Jefferson Co., Ky.	14c
Diorama of Life at Birthplace Cabin on Nolin Creek	14d
Lincoln's Birthplace Memorial Near Hodgenville, Ky.	14d
Home of Abe's Childhood on Knob Creek, Ky.	14d
Home of Lincoln's Youth Near Gentryville, Ind.	14e
Grave of Nancy Hanks Lincoln, Pigeon Creek, Ind.	14e
Two Silver Half-Dollars in Less Than a Day	14e
The Flatboat Trip to New Orleans in 1828	14e
Diorama of Life Within Lincoln's Indiana Home	14f
Lincoln Studies and Ciphers by the Firelight	14f
Diorama of the Lincoln Migration to Illinois	14g
Lincoln's Home on the Sangamon in Macon Co., Ill.	14g
Abraham Lincoln, the Rail-Splitter	14h
The Illinois Home of Thomas Lincoln's Later Years	14h

MAPS

Lincoln-Hanks Origins in England	16
Lincoln Homesteads in Massachusetts	16
First Lincoln-Hanks Migrations in America	24a
Migration Route Via Wilderness Road to Kentucky	36a
Lincoln Migration in 1816: Kentucky to Indiana	68
Lincoln Migration in 1830: Indiana to Illinois	68

ILLINOIS STATE HISTORICAL LIBRARY

ABRAHAM LINCOLN—PIONEER YOUTH
"At Twenty-one I Came to Illinois"
Statue at James Millikin University
By Fred M. Torrey

CHURCH HOMES OF THE LINCOLNS

"The Lincoln names—search anywhere—are found on church books where they lived." *Upper left*: The Lincolns' Parish Church at Hingham, Norfolk, England. *Upper right*: Progenitor Samuel Lincoln's "Old Ship" Church at Hingham, Mass., built in 1681 and in continuous use for more than 240 years. *Lower left*: Tom and Nancy Lincoln's Little Mound Church near Hodgenville, Ky. *Lower right*: Tom and Sarah's Pigeon Creek Church, which Tom helped build one mile south of their Spencer Co, Ind. home.

AMERICAN ANCESTRAL HOMES OF THE LINCOLNS

Upper left: Home of Mordecai Sr, son of Samuel Lincoln, built 1695 on North Scituate Promontory, Mass. *Upper right*: Home of Mordecai Jr., built 1733 in Berks Co, Exeter Township, Pa. *Lower left*: Jacob Lincoln's home, built 1800 on Linville Creek, Shenandoah Valley, Va., on land bought in 1768 by "Virginia John" Lincoln, Jacob's father. *Lower right*: Hughes Station, on Floyd's Creek, Jefferson Co., Ky., where Captain Abraham Lincoln was living while he built a cabin closeby.

Upper: CHICAGO HIST. SOC.   *Lower:* ILL. STATE HIST. LIBRARY

ABRAHAM LINCOLN'S BIRTHPLACE,
MEMORIAL, AND CHILDHOOD HOME

Upper: Diorama of life at the Nolin Creek cabin where Lincoln was born.
Lower left: Memorial Greek Temple which houses traditional log cabin birthplace.
Lower right: Knob Creek home of Abe's childhood. "My earliest recollection is of the Knob Creek place," said Lincoln.

Upper right: UNIV. OF ILL. LIBRARY. *Others:* ILL. STATE HIST. LIBRARY

LINCOLN'S HOME AND EXPERIENCES IN INDIANA

Upper left: Lincoln home near Gentryville, in Spencer Co., Ind., 1816-1830. *Upper right:* Nearby tomb of his mother, Nancy Hanks Lincoln. *Lower left:* Abe stared at two shining half-dollars, first he had ever earned so quickly. *Lower right:* Abe made his first flatboat trip to New Orleans in 1828.

Upper: CHICAGO HIST. SOC. *Lower:* ILL. STATE HIST. LIBRARY

INTERIOR OF LINCOLN'S HOME IN INDIANA

Upper: Sarah Bush Lincoln said, "I induced my husband to permit Abe to read and study at home ... At first he was not easily reconciled to it, but finally he too seemed willing to encourage him to a certain extent." *Lower:* Abe studying and ciphering by the firelight. "I'll study and get ready, and then, maybe, the chance will come."

Upper: CHICAGO HIST. SOC. *Lower:* ILL. STATE HIST. LIBRARY

THE LINCOLN'S MOVE TO ILLINOIS

Upper: Diorama of the migration-to-Illinois incident when Abe saved his little pup and, wading back, said "Here, Mammy, pet it up!" *Lower:* Lincoln's Macon Co. home, his first in Illinois. Dennis Hanks (shown, left) said, "Abe helped put up a cabin fur Tom on the Sangamon, clear fifteen acres fur corn an' split walnut rails to fence it in." John Hanks (shown, right) chose the cabin site.

ILLINOIS STATE HISTORICAL LIBRARY

AND SO THE PIONEER YOUTH BECAME A MAN
Upper: Lincoln, the Rail-Splitter, said that when seven years old he "had an ax put in his hands," but he did not intend that he should be *only* a rail-splitter!
Lower: Thomas Lincoln's last home was near Charleston, Ill. "I thought . . . t' move down to . . . Coles," he had said. So, there, on a place which Abe helped him buy and build, Thomas Lincoln lived out his remaining years.

LINCOLN HERITAGE
of
ABRAHAM LINCOLN

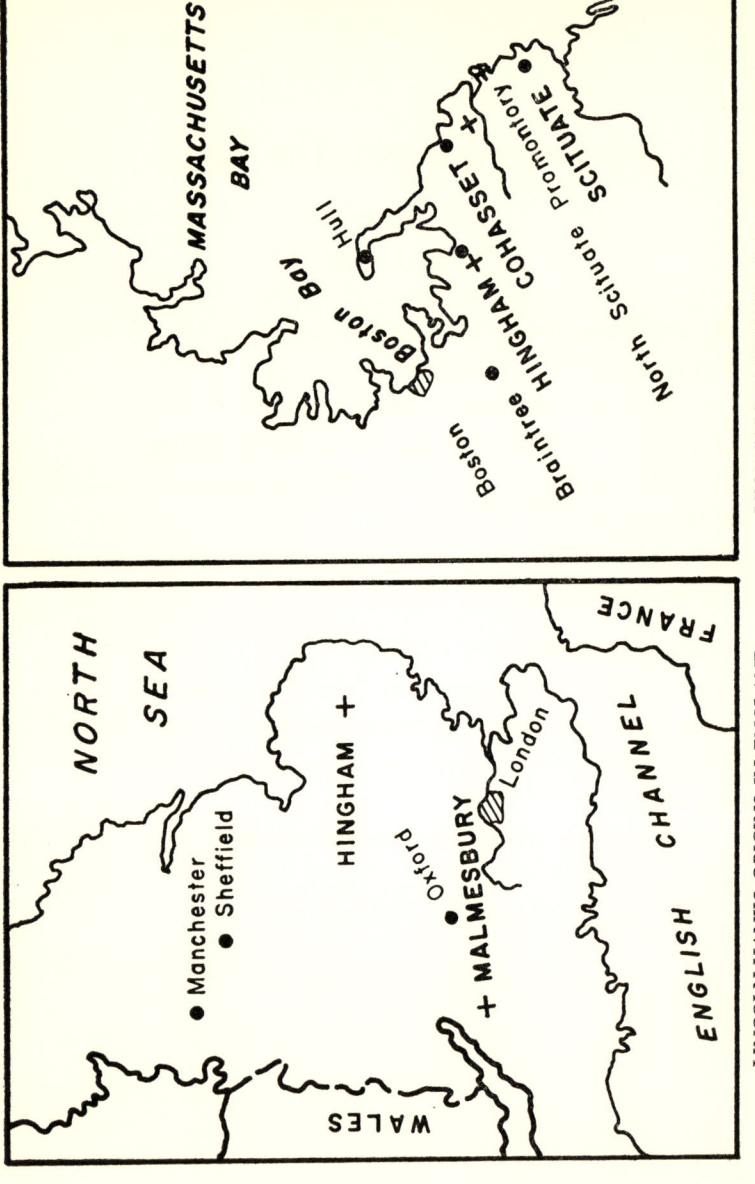

Specially drawn by Gerald Puckette for this Trilogy

LINCOLN-HANKS ORIGINS IN ENGLAND   LINCOLN HOMESTEADS IN MASSACHUSETTS

Left: Map of England showing HINGHAM, from whence Samuel Lincoln came to Massachusetts in 1637; and MALMESBURY, from whence Thomas Hanks came to Virginia in 1644. *Right:* Map of Massachusetts showing HINGHAM, home of Samuel

Abraham Lincoln: The Boy

GENEALOGY

Our world has always held an interest
In men of note, and justifiably
It searches wide throughout their ancestry
For brain and brawn that has the strength to best
All weaker men, and power to stand the test.
So, let us search the genealogy
Of Lincoln-Hanks, whose blood has come to be
A savior of America, the blest.

These seven generations I consign
To record here, and some were proved by notes
Direct from Lincoln's long ancestral line,
While others were secured from letter quotes,
Biographies, state papers, that combine
A song and sob within the readers' throats.

BRITAIN'S LOSS
1633

The Lincolns felt the cruel tyrant stings
In Hingham, England, many years before
Two brothers landed on New England's shore,*
Well schooled in trades. They were oppressed by kings
And priests, and sought escape on hopeful wings
By taking ship and braving ocean's roar
To reach America's wide-open door.
Free men dwell here, and freedom's bell still rings!

They felt the urge of patriot's clear view
That freedom lives, with God-inspired insight
To life and liberty, where men pursue
The way of happiness, which is their right!
All British craftsmen felt their wrongs and knew,
With Charles† upon the throne, that men must fight!

---

* Thomas and Daniel Lincoln. *See Addendum Note 1.*
† King Charles the First, of England.

THE FIRST LINCOLNS IN AMERICA
1633

The Lincoln trait of mind was always known
To reason each thing out till one could see
All trends and bents of meaning's tracery,
And thus Tom Lincoln reasoned on his own:
"With Tory rule and Charles upon the throne,
A craftsman's pay is small.* Now as for me,
I'll take my chance in some new colony
In far America, where hopes are grown."

He had with him his younger brother, Dan,
And soon they owned both land and home and grew
Content. They daily met the Indian
And sought his confidence. And when the two
Were joined by Sam,† the stalwart Lincoln[3] clan
America has famed, had its debut.

---

* Political tyranny added to religious unrest had upset England's economy.
† Samuel Lincoln, brother of Tom and Dan.[2]

SAM LINCOLN IN MASSACHUSETTS
1637-1690

Though Sam was in his teens,[*] he had been schooled
And was well trained to work the weaver's trade,
Yet realized that craftsmen were not paid
A living wage, that Charles the First befooled
His Parliament: *gave them no voice,* but ruled
And governed all as tyrants do, with aid
Or privilege to none; *his will* was made
The law while all the people's rights were pooled.[†]

Unhampered in America, Sam's dream
Of owning land and home and family
Developed through a steady growing stream
Of work and clan. In time he came to be
Progenitor of him[§] who would redeem
A troubled nation bound by slavery.

---

[*] Sam was 18 when he arrived in 1637 as weaver Frances Lawes' apprentice.[4]

[†] No meetings of Parliament had been permitted by Charles the First since 1629.

[§] Sam was President Abraham Lincoln's great-great-great-great-grandfather. In 1690, "old Sam Linkoln dyed of the smallpox."[5]

THE LINCOLN CLAN
1637-1865

From Sam to Abe, six generations saw
An Abraham. The President, who took
His seat in 'sixty-one, short-schooled, save book
And eagerness to learn in marveled awe,
Had wrought a love of wisdom that would draw
A nation's trust to him. One backward look
Reveals in Sam and Abe no will to brook
Misrule, or loss of people's rights at law.

Down through the Lincoln clan there flowed rich blood
Of patriots declaring, "Right makes might!"
It stood for honor in its time: bore thud
And brunt of wars, maintaining church* and right
With reverence for God, its growing bud
Unfolding into bloom of purest white.

---

* Sam Lincoln's and his sons' money helped to build and maintain "Old Ship Church" at Hingham, Massachusetts. Erected in 1681, it is the oldest church building in America in continuous use for more than 240 years.[6]

MORDECAI, SON OF SAMUEL
1657-1727

Sam's bachelor brother, Dan, had died[7] and willed
The whole of his estate to Sam who bought
More land and built a house, where then he brought
A bride. His "Martha" stood with him, befrilled
In lace and veil and took the vow. She filled
His home with love, and many children taught:
One, Mordecai by name, whose strength was wrought
At blacksmith forge, was known to be well skilled.

He, then, found Sarah Jones across the bay
And married her; and their first child was named
Young Mordecai, the next was Abraham.*
A sawmill, grist and forge could never stay
Old Mordecai; his work in iron was famed,†
And won him honest wealth there by the dam.

---

* This is the *first Abraham* in the Lincoln line. He was named thus for his mother's father, Abraham Jones.[8]

† One of America's first ironmongers who made iron from ore he smelted.[9]

THE BROKEN FAMILY

When Sarah died, Old Mordecai took wife,*
A widow, Mary Chapin of Braintree,
And built a house for her that all may see
Today in Scituate.† But whether strife
By bickering and nagging spleen was rife,
Young Mordecai and Abraham went free
To seek some other place where each could be
Content to build anew his unleashed life.

Perhaps religious freedom, rights of poor
And rich, with thoughts these differences wrought,
Had sent them out to find and learn by tour
New Jersey's gratis land for homes they sought.
Here bickerings would cease with rights secure,
Through England's pledge—to worship as one thought.§

---

* In 1701-1702.

† Well preserved and lived in after 200 years. *See Addendum Note 10. See map* on p. 16, this volume.

§ England promised "free liberty of conscience without molestation or disturbance in the way of worship."

MORDECAI JR. IN NEW JERSEY

America, where freedom has its reign,
Was sought by those relentlessly oppressed;
But these, by ironclad rules, soon caused unrest
That branded freedom's land with blackened stain.
When England advertised New Jersey's plain
And hill, where men felt free and doubly blessed
To worship God as conscience dictates best,
Men rushed to find that place where peace was gain.

Thus Mordecai and Abraham had found
Asylum in this land with hope's array,
And built a forge on Buckhorn Manor ground.
The owner had a daughter, Hannah, gay
Young heiress, prettiest in miles around,
Who loved and married Mordecai one day.*

---

* Mordecai Jr. was living in New Jersey as early as September 14, 1714 married to Hannah Saltar, only daughter of Richard Saltar, owner of 2,100 acres of land just north of Middletown known as Buckhorn Manor.[11]

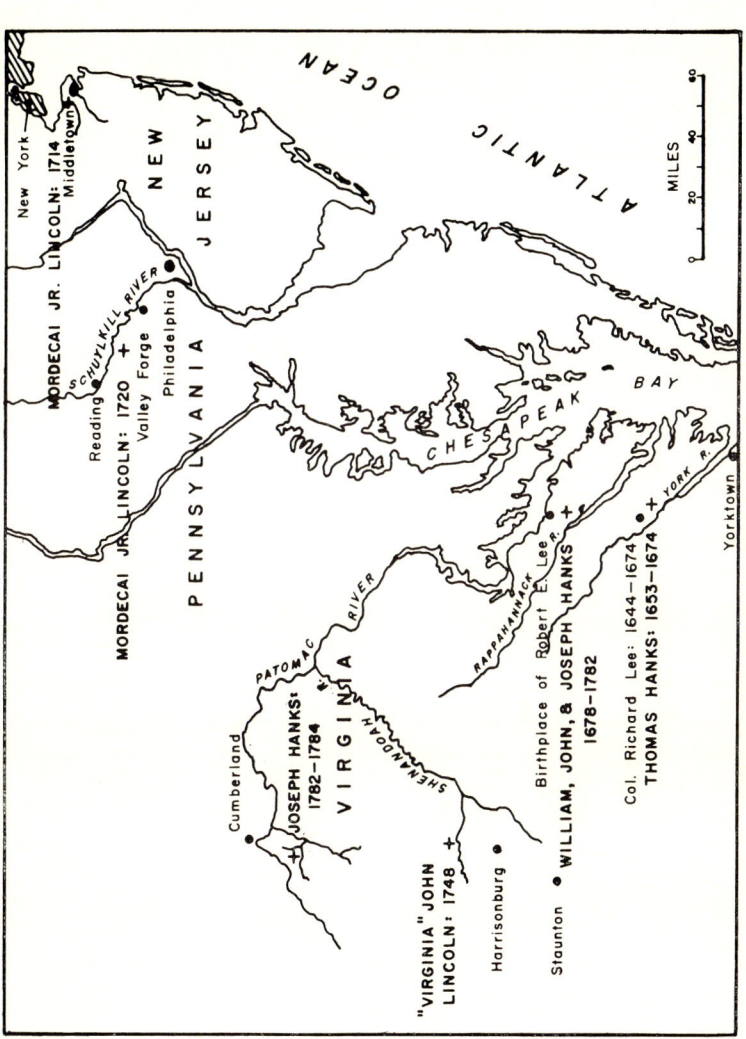

Specially drawn by Gerald Puckette for this Trilogy

FIRST LINCOLN-HANKS MIGRATIONS IN AMERICA

(a) Mordecai Lincoln's son, Mordecai Jr, moved to Buckhorn Manor, near Middletown, NEW JERSEY, then to Berks Co., near Reading, PENNSYLVANIA. His son, John, moved to Linville Cr., Shenandoah Valley, VIRGINIA. (b) After Thomas Hanks' death during Indian uprisings, William was found on the safer north side of Rappahannock R. After Lucy's trouble in Richmond Co. Joseph Hanks moved to Mike's Run on Patterson's Cr, Hampshire Co., Va.

MORDECAI JR.'S TWO WIVES

But Hannah Lincoln's years were short; one day
She bade her family a long good-bye.
Her children needed care, so Mordecai,
In time, brought Mary home as wife.* Her way
Was law to honor, reverence, obey;
God's truth and right failed not to satisfy.
She cared for Hannah's five and bore, with sigh,
Her own three sons, and had no time to play.

For Hannah left four daughters, and son John,
Who helped young Mary till they all were wed.
Then, left alone,† brave Mary struggled on
To raise her stalwart sons, who soon were led—
When colonies bade tyranny begone—
To give their service "where the sands ran red."§

---

* Hannah likely died soon after February 1727. Mary was perhaps the daughter of Andrew Robeson of Amity, Pennsylvania.[12]

† Mary's husband, Mordecai, died in 1736.

§ In the American Revolution, serving as stated in *Addendum Note 13*.

MORDECAI JR. MOVES TO PENNSYLVANIA*

Because New Jersey lacked facility
For marketing, shrewd Mordecai, allured
By Pennsylvania's offerings, secured
Three hundred acres there; moved family,
And built a house—a show place yet to see.†
"Mord" was a leader in his town, matured
In reasoning and judgement, who adjured
A tolerance all felt must come to be.

His life was short, death came at forty-nine.
Four sons were left, four charming daughters, too.
They tilled his thousand acres, rich and fine,
For each child shared a portion as its due.§
His home, well built, is still an honored shrine.
Here lived a man beloved, sincere and true.

---

* By 1720, where he found better transportation, water power and iron ore.[14] *See map* on p. 24, this volume.

† It is a Brittany-like house with date stone "ML 1733", steep roof, plaster walls, deep basement, small servants' quarters, red sandstone terrace, set on a hillside above a brook at Exeter, Berks County, Pennsylvania.[15]

§ The New Jersey half to Hannah's children, the Pennsylvania half to Mary's sons.

ENGLAND'S UNJUST TAX
1773

A British ship had entered Boston bay.
Excitement then prevailed, for all could see
Injustice brewing for the colony.
With goods *forced on them,* with a *tax* to pay,
"A score of days to clear"—all felt dismay!*
Discussions everywhere made folks agree
That Boston should refuse the tax-bound tea,
When leaders met to act the final day.

But Tory sentiment, in some, ran high;
Through mother love, and deference to king,
Some hesitated rather than defy.
Thus, patriots feared loyalists would bring
Disaster to their planning to deny
The tea an entry with its harsh tax-sting.†

---

* For "if the ships were not unloaded within twenty days the custom-house officers had the right to unload them. The nineteenth day came, and unless something decisive was done the tea would be brought ashore at sunrise the next morning."[16]

† "Taxation without representation."

TEA IN PAPPY'S SHOES
1773

Sam Adams likely said, "Go to the room
Behind the printing press; we'll find a way*
To rid ourselves of tax the British lay
Upon our colonies." All sensed a gloom
Lest their Selectmen in town hall should doom
Their rights, by an agreement there to pay
The tax, forever making them the prey
Of kings and wealth, forever some lord's groom.

These tradesmen met. One whispered angrily,
"That tea-ship's in the bay. Let us disguise
As Indians and dump it in the sea!"
And so their deed was wrought!† At dawn, bright eyes
Of Lincoln's little son found fresh green tea
In Pappy's work-worn shoes—and just looked wise.

---

* Adams is said to have signaled the way finally chosen.[17]

† Amos Lincoln, great-great-grandson of progenitor Samuel Lincoln, "took part in the 'Boston Tea Party' . . . [and] it is said, at family prayers that night [Mr. Crafts, to whom Amos was apprenticed,] prayed for 'the young men out on their perilous errand.'" Amos, an artillery captain in the Revolutionary army, was husband of Paul Revere's daughter.[18]

THE LINCOLNS AND THE BOONES

Down in the town of Exeter, Squire Boone
Had settled. George and Dan,* the proud old Squire's
Two sons, were reared and taught by crackling fires
That burned on hearths to welcome all. There, croon
Of lullabies was heard for ten. The moon
Shone on their home and night wind's drowsy choirs
Sang happy serenade that love inspires:
Two Lincolns married Boones,† so goes the rune.

The Lincolns lived across the field upon
A hill, where all the neighbors met to pray,
Before they built a church, or else to con
The news from colonies—the unjust fray
Of Tory rule; and Dan, sometimes till dawn,
Told of the land down new Kentucky way.

---

* *The* Daniel Boone, famous Kentucky pioneer. The elder Boone's name was Squire. He did not hold a squire's office.

† William and Anne Boone, own cousins of Daniel Boone, married respectively Sarah and Abraham Lincoln, children of Mordecai Jr.[19]

SHENANDOAH VIRGINIA
1768

The oldest son of Mordecai was John.
His father's gift, three hundred acres, he
Had sold, and moved his stock and family
To "Shenandoah's vale." Content grew wan—
The "Westward Ho!" made pioneers move on.
John bought six hundred acres, broad and free,
With vistas of rich soil, clear stream and tree.
Here Becky's wifely grace was paragon.*

The neighbors were twelve miles or more apart.
John's land was bordered by the thoroughfare
That led from north to south and west. A mart
Nearby, provided all the valley there
With tools and cloth, and news that chilled the heart:
Of British tyrannies, which left despair.

---

* John married, in 1743, Rebecca Flowers Morris, a widow with one son; sold his 300 acres in New Jersey in 1748, and in 1768 bought this 600 bordering Linville's creek in Shenandoah Valley north of Harrisonburg, Rockingham County, Virginia.[20]
See map on p. 24, this volume.

INDUSTRIAL INDEPENDENCE

The English tax on everything had made
The people pause and think what course was best*
For individuals whose wills have blessed
Mankind, creating things their vision stayed.
These hardy men with craftman-skill had laid
A firm foundation that would stand the test
Industrial development possessed.
Designs they wrought well-patterned later trade.

The Lincolns fashioned iron screws and nails,
Strong hinges, skillets, pots and pewter ware.
They wove their cloth, made cabinets and pails,
And tables, chairs and plates of wood. And there
Were tools for every need along the trails.
Since scourged by tax, men met their needs by dare.

---

* Samuel Adams and others "bound themselves 'to eat nothing, drink nothing, wear nothing' imported from England..."[21]

WAR! WAR! WAR!
1775

The way that Britain viewed her colonies
Was as a Lord for underlings. Offense
Was felt. She did not counsel with them, hence
When taxes were imposed, indignities
Were sure to cause resentment, as with bees
When robbed. The colonists rebelled through sense
Of rancor, and with all their confidence
In Britain gone, they *fought her* grim *decrees*.

And when the war had come, men filled the ranks:
The Lincolns,* Crowders, Rankins everywhere
Fought bravely for their cause beside the Hanks
And Wears through darkest hours, with faith in prayer;
And Frenchmen fighting bravely by the Yanks
Made courage permeate the vibrant air.

---

* The records show 335 Revolutionary soldiers named Lincoln.[22]

"VIRGINIA JOHN"
1788

When death took John* away from life's estate,
He left behind nine children trained to be
A blessing to their own community,
For all of them were taught to tolerate
Men's varied ways, to work and to create
True values, and to live courageously—
To worship God, and strive to keep men free.
And thus John lived his life, inviolate.†

Today, in all these parts, the Lincoln name
Is still revered and loved for strength and grace.
You hear, "I'm Mordecai!" or "Tom!" or "Sam!"
As shouted by a boy in wild acclaim.
You look and feel a start, for in his face
You find the features loved in Abraham.

---

* Oldest son of Mordecai Jr. of Exeter, Pennsylvania. See p. 30 of this book, also *map* on p. 24.

† Miss Tarbell,[23] after reviewing New Jersey, Pennsylvania and Virginia records pertaining to this great-grandfather of President Lincoln, concludes that he was undoubtedly a courageous, energetic, level-headed and tolerant man of fidelity who, though prosperous in business, was above all devout and careful in all things.

THE LINCOLN GIFT

The Lincoln families have left a son,
Or daughter, trained to serve in every state
Where they have lived. Through faithfulness, they rate
Among the best as citizens. No one
Has shown a greater leadership, and none
Has given more to aid and extricate
America from wrongs* that violate
The rights of men, which noble courage spun.

They were the civic leaders, men of prayer.
They were the settlers' vanguard, bold and free.
They helped destroy the tax on British ware.
As Governors, the Lincolns numbered three—†
And Abe became our President. All share
Our gratitude and love wholeheartedly.

---

* Might against right.

† Levi Lincoln, great-great-grandson of progenitor Samuel Lincoln, was Governor of Massachusetts, as was also his son, Levi Jr.; and Enoch, another son of Levi Sr., was Governor of Maine.[24]

ABRAHAM WOOS BATHSHEBA

Young Abraham, the oldest of John's sons,
Was set to guard the homesteads and the land
From roving Indians. His faithful band
Of brave militia, with their knives and guns,
Made safe the homes of Shenandoah's runs.
In leisure hours he sought a maiden's hand,
Bathsheba Herring's. But her father's stand
Was firm and classed them both as simpletons.

"In fact," he gasped, "I'll disinherit you!"*
But "Sheba's" love for Abraham was strong,
So they were wed.† John blessed their happy coup—
Conveyed them land§ to heal her father's wrong—
So that they prospered and contentment grew,
And children filled their home with joyful song.

---

* Bathsheba's vain "father looked with scorn on the alliance, and gave his daughter the choice of giving up her lover or being disinherited."[25]

† "No vestige of proof has been found that his marriage in 1770 was not to Bathsheba. She was Abraham's wife in 1780 and in 1782 accompanied him to Kentucky." She was still his wife when he died.[26]

§ The deed conveys "Two Hundred and Ten Acres."[27]

ABRAHAM COMMISSIONED CAPTAIN

The Northwest had a need for trained men who
Well understood the duties of a guard
For settlers and their rights. The work was hard,
But Abraham, John's son, held well this view;
So Old Virginia, feeling honors due,
Had made him *Captain*.* He then like a bard
Of old, set forth with song that soon was marred,
In "Ol' Kaintuck", by red men's wild halloo.

He and a party traversed Blue Ridge gap
At Cumberland, then over hills they went
Along the road called "Wilderness,"† with cap
And trigger set for Indians intent
On war. Bathsheba held Tom on her lap,
Unknowing his son would be President!

---

* As early as 1770, Abraham Lincoln, grandfather of President Lincoln, was a captain in the Virginia militia.[28]

† "In the first half of 1782 . . . Abraham and Bathsheba Lincoln, with their five children, left Rockingham for Kentucky." The Wilderness Road, first marked by Daniel Boone, in 1775, was a pack horse trail until 1796 when Kentucky made it a wagon road. Much of it followed an old Indian "warriors' path."[29]

MIGRATION ROUTE VIA WILDERNESS ROAD TO KENTUCKY

Map of the Wilderness Road showing route traveled in 1782 by Captain Abraham Lincoln, his wife Bathsheba, and their children—including Thomas, who later became the father of President Abraham Lincoln. Joseph Hanks and his family likely followed this same route about two years later as they moved to Rolling Fork of Pottinger's Cr, Nelson Co., Kentucky.

KENTUCKY
1784

Virginia had acquired Kentucky lands
From Indians, who took the contract fee
And then refused to leave. They failed to see
The rights of those who came in ardent bands
Around the Blue Ridge range with eager hands
To till the soil and make a home, to be
Kept safe by pledges of security.*
Thus came the Lincolns with their trust demands.

But when they reached the fort[†] where they were sent,
They found they must reside within its walls
Of barricades, because the red men's bent
Was driving white men off the land with brawls
And cruel theft of scalps. Now, time has spent
These wild attacks and draped them with its palls.

---

* Virginia had pledged, to homesteaders in Kentucky, security of land transfers, as well as forts for personal protection from the Indians.

† Hughes' Station, on Floyd's Creek, Jefferson County, Kentucky. (In 1784 the entire Kentucky territory, with a population of 30,000, had but 18 houses outside its 52 stockades, or stations.)[30]

LINCOLN BUYS KENTUCKY LAND

Because they liked the soil in Jefferson,*
The Lincolns sold their Shenandoah land
And bought twelve hundred acres.† Here they planned
And built a hut close by the fort.§ When done,
It would be home. Meantime, they had begun
To till the earth and clear the wooded stand,
Though furtive red men skulked nearby and scanned
Their every move with spleen that hate had spun.

They held for Captain Lincoln, bitter scorn.
His shot was sure, his aim was true! They craved
His scalp to deck their belts. And to adorn
Their savage arrogance, their malice laved
Its sharpest arrows; bitterness had borne:
"His scalp upon our belts, our lands are saved!"

---

* Jefferson *County*, Kentucky.

† In 1780; 800 acres on Green River, in Lincoln County (named for General Benjamin Lincoln); 400 acres in Jefferson County, on Long Run Fork of Floyd's Creek, close by Hughes' Station.[31] *See map* on p. 36, this volume.

§ Investigators have discovered what is thought to be ruins of Hughes' Station and the unfinished Lincoln cabin, *not more than 400 feet apart.*[32]

CAPTAIN LINCOLN
1784

He quelled uprisings, worked for friendly ties
Red men refused until he *forced* a calm!
To eastern men, the land was like a psalm
Intoned at eventide, a place to prize.
He bought two thousand acres* where blue skies
Arched high above Green River and no qualm
Of fear was felt. His world was in his palm,
As growing grain gave pleasure to his eyes.

It grew abundantly, with yearly yield
That far surpassed his fondest hope or dream.
Yet as he tended well his growing field,
Well watered by the lavish purling stream,
He overlooked that malice never healed
In red men's hearts, but burst like angry steam.

---

* ". . . the actual extent of land in the name of [Captain] Abraham Lincoln at the time of his death was 5,544 acres. A considerable estate for a 'drifting, roaming people [whom authors have claimed was] struggling with poverty.' "[33]

REVENGE
May, 1786

One morning when small Thomas saw his dad
Start to the field to plant his corn, he cried,
"Let me come, Pap, and drop seeds by your side!"
"What, you! Ha! Yo's too young, my little lad.
Yo's all but seven yet. When you has had
Mo' time t' grow, I'll turn t' you with pride!
But, Sonny-boy, now you all run an' hide
Yo' se'f in Mammy's breast!" Tom's eyes grew sad.

His wayward feet sought shelter by a hedge,
And there he followed close his father's trail,
Unseen. A shot rang from the timber's edge.
Tom saw his father reel and fall. His wail
Was heard: "My Pappy's kilt upon th' ledge!"
The one on guard was quickened to assail.*

---

* Captain Lincoln had left his oldest son, Mordecai, age 15, on guard with a rifle, at their unfinished log cabin where he had a good view of his father as he worked. Mordecai witnessed his father's death and sent his younger brother, Josiah, age 13, to rouse the fort to come to his rescue.[34]

RESCUE

Tom scampered quickly to his father's side.
He knew no fear, but felt a frantic love
As, tearfully dismayed, he bent above
The prostrate form. He heard a heavy stride,
Saw scalping knife gleam in the air. He cried
On feeling fingers grip his arm and shove
And drag him, helpless as a turtledove
Ensnared, toward woodland gloom that fortified.

Another shot! Tom felt the human band
That bound his arm release its hold, and saw
A red man fall in death upon the sand.
He ran in fright back toward the hut. In awe
His brother met him, rescue gun in hand,
As other red men hurried to withdraw.*

---

* Mordecai had killed his father's slayer as the Indian was dragging Tommy away.[35]

BEREAVEMENT

Bathsheba sat alone beside her dead,
And sadly thought, "How can my oldest son,
Not yet fifteen, complete our house, or run
The farm? This needs an older hand. Instead,
We'll move to Washington* where friends have said:
'We all have work their hands can do. Each one
Can earn a bit to help along and none
Shall want. For work, we'll give them food and bed.'"

The Berrys, Thompsons and the Hanks were in
The party with the Lincolns. Friendships weigh
The loyalties as marks of genuine.
She joined these friends,† and for their part each day,
Her sons did neighbors' chores till they could win,
Through needed strength, man's status and his pay.

---

* Washington *County*. *See* Springfield on *map,* p. 36.

† But not "until she had harvested the pathetic crop which her husband was sowing when he was killed; she was still living on Long Run in September, 1786." For on the 18th of that month "Widow Lincoln" is included on a subscription list as donor of a gun for an expedition against the Indians.[36]

COUSIN HANANIAH LINCOLN*

Now Hananiah Lincoln had become
Well known throughout the state, was said to be
Quite rich in land.† His business eye could see
A fortune in the soil. He purchased some,
Then traded it for more. His premium. . .
The confidence of all for honesty!
When "Cousin Abraham" met tragedy,
Good Hananiah's heart was crushed and numb.

Concerned to aid, he sought his cousin's folk,
And helped them choose and plan the future way
Of life that satisfied their needs. His cloak
Of love most likely counseled them to stay
Among her friends where all would bear her yoke.
None could do less in Lincoln mold of clay!

---

* We know that Hananiah enjoyed the trust of Captain Abraham since he had assisted Hananiah with extensive loans, and that therefore Hananiah had reason to feel deeply indebted to him and especially obligated to his widow, Bathsheba. Hananiah was the eldest son of Abraham's Uncle Thomas and Aunt Elizabeth of Reading, Pennsylvania.[37]

† 8,972½ acres, according to Daniel Boone's Survey Book.[38]

COUSIN HANANIAH TELLS ABOUT THE WAR
September 11, 1777

Now once, when Hananiah Lincoln came
To visit "Sheba" and her family,
They sat before a blazing fire and he
Explained the war* that raged, and "who's to blame."
His words: "You know it's not a childish game!
No, sir! We colonists saw need to free
Ourselves, and so declared our liberty!
That's why I joined, to smash Old Britain's claim!

And I, with Washington and others there,†
Fought on the Brandywine with will and might!
Some men were shoeless, had but rags to wear,
No pay to send to wives in helpless plight
At home; and yet, these men were like wild bear
In every battle fought for human right!"

---

* The American Revolutionary War.

† Among the "others" were Crowders and Wears,[39] Rankins and Blackburns, ancestors of the author.

FRANCE RECOGNIZES AMERICA
1777

Tom asked, "And did you win at Brandywine?"
"No, Tom, we lost; but scored at Bennington
And Saratoga! Guess what next was done!
You can't? Well, Frenchmen had things well in line:
They sent us guns and men, and dared define
Us as *'a nation'!* We could not have won
But for the help of France. You see, my son,
France had long warred with England 'cross the brine!*

And France well knew to break the British hold
On us would cause her loss of colonies,
And hurt her most. So, France sent ships and gold
And guns to us." "But guns have stings like bees,"
Said Tom. "Weren't you afraid?" "No, Tom, man's mold
Is worthless when he has no liberties!"

---

* France felt chagrin and had suffered much loss in her defeat by England's navy in the Seven Year's War of 1756-1763, so to get even she gave aid to England's American colonies. After the colonists' great victory at Saratoga in 1777, France acknowledged the independence of the United States and "sent the flower of France to fight beside the Americans."

BATHSHEBA LINCOLN

Too much cannot be said in praise of her
Who bravely faced the future of that day;
She with the five young children, far away
From kindred help. She never voiced demur;
The courage she revealed became a spur
That daily sent the young to work for pay.
She taught them how to live, let live, and pray.
The home was theirs, and no man could deter.*

The heir-at-law, a *minor,* eldest son,
Could not divide the Lincoln land estate;†
Her boys she hoped could learn some trade. But one,
Young Tom, "worked out" till he was twenty-eight,
At twenty-five he purchased land§ and gun,
Before he had made choice of trades or mate.

---

* Bathsheba did not marry again.

† Tom's brother Mordecai, because of law suits to clear and because he was only 15 when his father died, was delayed in dividing the land estate. He sold portions, and may have paid Josiah and Tom, in 1797 and 1803, respectively.[40]

§ In 1803, he purchased the Mill Creek farm of 238 acres, 8 miles north of Elizabethtown in Hardin County, Kentucky, near where in 1801 his sister Nancy Lincoln Brumfield located.[41]

HANKS HERITAGE
of
ABRAHAM LINCOLN

THOMAS HANKS AN ENGLISH PRISONER
1643

Tom Hanks of Malmesbury, an English town,
Had fought* in Cromwell's Civil War, and few
Fought harder to oppose King Charles. Not through,
The King shipped prisoners, by "rights of Crown,"
Across the sea.† Tom shared the King's grim frown—
Was sent to servitude, with men he knew.
They worked in forests, mills and fields, and drew
The hardest toil, a fate without renown.

One Captain Fowke, a British merchant, sold
Some prisoners among the colonies;
And of this lot was Tom, exchanged for gold,
To slave through summer's heat and winter's freeze.
The tyrant's rule grew worse, until his hold
Had ceased in death;§ then, England found some ease.

---

* 1642-1643.

† Wishing to be rid of all who opposed him, the King gave to "Thomas Fowke, merchant of Westmoreland County . . . fifty acres of land for transporting . . . into Virginia, one . . . Thomas Hanks." Fowke also thus possessed Tom Hanks' services to be sold to some colonist for gold.[42]

§ King Charles the First was beheaded in 1649.

THOMAS HANKS
1644-1676

It seems Tom worked out his apprenticeship,*
For by year sixteen hundred fifty-three
The records show him buying land, and free—
A large proprietor,† secure from grip
Of fear. But Indians then dared to slip
Back into native haunts, revengefully,
And Berkeley failed to aid the colony
Till Bacon sought rebellion§ as a whip.

Not since that date has trace been found of Hanks;
His life it seems went up in smoke and blood
That angry red men left. The neighbors' ranks
Were thinned, plantations overrun, and thud
Of tomahawks were felt upon the banks
Of Rappahannock's gory swirling flood.

---

* 7 to 14 years. Tom Hanks was likely indentured for only 7 years.

† 2,481 acres.[43] *See map* on p. 24, this volume.

§ Bacon's Rebellion, a Virginia settlers' uprising precipitated in 1676 by an Indian outbreak which British-appointed Governor William Berkeley refused to take adequate measures to suppress. First, a band of volunteers led by one of the planters, Nathaniel Bacon, repulsed the Indians, then, accused of insubordination for having done so, they revolted against the aristocratic and irresponsible government of their accuser, Sir Berkeley.

WILLIAM HANKS

An exodus from Gloucester* came when
The war was through, for all had come to see
The Rappahannock gave security
To homes built by its northern bank. Here, then,
Was found a William Hanks among the men;
A stalwart youth, with spouse.† Most likely he
Was one of Thomas Hanks' own family,
Who built across from Tom's, within a glen.

And Sarah Woodbridge was his wife who bore
Him sons whose names were William, Luke and John,
And blessed with health and strength of limb, they tore
The woodland's tangled growth apart. Hereon
They built a large estate; and from the lore
Of time, true worth was in their lexicon.

---

* Gloucester County, Virginia, was south and west of the Rappahannock River.

† It is presumed that William, who made his living as a carpenter, found it not too difficult to adjust to his wife Sarah's desire not to leave the home place where she had been born, so he moved across the river to join her there in what later became Richmond County.[44]

JOHN AND JOSEPH HANKS

When William's sons grew up, their legacy
In Richmond County was the fertile ground
Their father had acquired. And they had found
It good. John married Catherine, and he
Amassed a large estate and family.*
One of their sons was Joseph,† sane and sound,
Who when of age had learned love's fetters bound
His neighbor's daughter as his wife, Ann Lee.

And Joseph and his flock remained upon
The land in Richmond that his "Grandpap Bill
Had bought and cleared, and which his father, John,
Had added to," said some who lived there still.
Then came his crash of pride. His joy was gone.
His Lucy wore a scarlet "A" as frill.§

---

* This John Hanks is the great-great-grandfather of President Lincoln. He and his wife Catherine had nine children, one of them Joseph.[45]

† Joseph was administrator of Catherine's rather large estate. He married Ann Lee, of the family of Virginia Lees who gave us Robert E. Lee. Joseph and Ann *Lee* Hanks were President Lincoln's great-grandparents.[46]

§ "A" for adultery.

JOSEPH MOVES TO KENTUCKY
1782-1787

The shock had torn Joe's heart and crushed his pride,
And gossip's tongue had added to his shame
For Hanks and Lees all treasured grace of name.
Joe felt their happiness could not abide
In Richmond County and moved out.[47] With guide
He sought a home in "Old Kaintuck." No blame
Could surely rest upon them there, to maim
His children's worth when he and Ann had died.

Joe bought an hundred fifty acre run
On Rolling Fork in Nelson County, meant
As farm and home, and purchased for his son,[48]
"Who ought to farm," he said, "and know content."
But, "where birds fly their tails will follow," one
Has said, and gossip's tongue wagged, evil-bent.

ACCUSERS

Joe brought young Lucy* and her child with him.
Again, the neighbors talked suspiciously:
"So young to be deceived! And *who* is *he?*
The baby's name is *Nancy*—cherubim,
If ever there was one! Too bad to dim
Its future with *her* wrong!" No charity
For thoughtless youth or its mistake! No plea
For her who bears the shame alone, though grim!

Misunderstanding was her lot. So gay
Her dreams, her eager constant yen to glow
In admiration's gleam had made her stray.
Yet there were some who dared declare, "Although
Her sin is great, in fairness folks should say,
'Her's is a human flaw as all must know.' "

---

* Lucy, eldest daughter of Joseph and Ann, was born about 1766 and likely died about 1825. The father of her Nancy is still unknown. She gave her parents much chagrin until 1790 when she married Henry Sparrow, a Revolutionary soldier, and began a new and honorable life. Two of the eight children she bore him were ministers of the gospel.[49]

SOME HANKS HISTORY
1790-1796

Young Henry Sparrow, patriot, had come
To dwell near Joe Hanks' home. His urge to claim
The hand of Lucy, who had borne the shame
Of gossip's stigma and its odium,
Won Joe's consent. And they through life heard strum
Of peace and happiness, each day the same.
They farmed their fields, and kindness was a game
To them—with charity as premium.

When Lucy's father died, within a year
Young Joe decided not to farm; so he
Assigned his land to brother Will and said,
"I'll make the woodcraft art my life career."
Joe's mother, Ann, then went back East to see
Her son, and Betsy Hanks and Tom were wed.*

---

* (a) Lucy Hanks married Henry Sparrow in 1790.

(b) Joseph Hanks Sr. died in 1793, and Joe Jr. opened his woodcraft shop in Elizabethtown after he had assigned his farm inheritance to William Hanks in 1794.

(c) Ann Lee Hanks, Joe's mother went to Virginia to visit her eldest son, Tom, where she died; and, in 1796, Elizabeth Hanks—sister of Nancy, Joe Jr., Will and Lucy—married Thomas Sparrow.[50]

THOMAS AND ELIZABETH SPARROW

Tom Sparrow's home was without child to play
And romp as children do about the room,
So they took Nancy* to dispell the gloom.
Throughout the years, all loved her gentle way,
For she was taught God's love for all who stray;
Was taught design, to sew, and work the loom.
She learned the joy that comes in youthful bloom,
And power of faith that overcomes dismay.

Well sheltered, clothed and fed, she learned to read[†]
Good books, but sewing was her special art.
She won in spinning contests by her speed
And knew the skill of forming hem and dart.
Thus Nancy sewed for all who were in need,
And gained the grateful love of every heart.

---

* "Nancy was not less than twelve years of age when she went to live with this uncle and aunt."[51]

† Though Nancy was "a ready reader," she had not been taught to write. (Documents discovered bear only her X, not her signature.)[51]

TOM LINCOLN LEARNS A TRADE

The trying years Tom spent in working through
Necessity to earn his keep each day
In nearby homes and fields, or far away,
Revealed his need of discipline. He knew
At twenty-eight he lacked the skill to do
The better tasks, he had no trade to stay
His restless hands and win a worthy pay;
And so he sought a friend with this in view.

There in the shop of Joseph Hanks he saw
The finer workings of the woodcraft art.
Joe stopped just long enough to share a law:
"To learn to make a cabinet, each *part*
Is *mastered* and is *made without a flaw*,
To gain the skill." Tom smiled, "When do I start?"*

---

* (a) "It was in the shop of her [Nancy's] uncle, Joseph Hanks, at Elizabethtown in Hardin County, that he [Tom] essayed to learn the trade" of carpenter and cabinetmaker.

(b) Among the things he learned to make were coffins, cabinets, window sash and door frames.

(c) " 'Tom had the best set of tools in what was then and now is Washington County [and was] a good carpenter . . .' a skilled craftsman."[52]

TOM AND NANCY FALL IN LOVE

The Berry home was neighbor to the Hanks';
Here Nancy worked.* She loved Tom Lincoln, too.
He took her to each party's rendezvous,
And at the church he chose her from the ranks
Of gay young girls and boasted, "Now, I banks
Her 'ginst 'em all fo' beauty! An' she's true!"
On nights when there was nothing else to do
They sat and sparked, she laughing at his pranks.

And thus he courted her, his lady fair;
He won her love and pledge to be his bride.
They planned within a year they would be wed.†
Tom owned some acres and a house;§ though bare
And small, it had a fireplace on one side.
They hoped and dreamed of happiness ahead.

---

* Nancy sewed for Mrs. Richard Berry, her lifelong friend.

† What girl in Nancy's day or this would not envy her when Tom came courting? A militiaman, an Indian fighter, a minor political appointee, owner of a good farm, choosing also to add cabinetwork as his trade; a mature man of wide travel and experience, one of integrity and honor.[53]

§ The 238-acre Mill Creek farm he had bought three years before when age 25, and he owned a house and lot in Elizabethtown.

THE WEDDING
June 12, 1806

The wedding in the Berry home* was grand
And long remembered as a gay affair,
For all the folks from miles around were there
To see the marriage Tom and Nancy planned.
Young Parson Jesse Head, with his own hand,
Wrote up the nuptial bond, a treasure rare
To see, that still is shown with pious air
In Springfield's† Courthouse, shared at pride's demand.

The wedding dinner was the fate that day.§
The pretty bride blushed furiously when kissed!
They feasted and they danced the hours away,
And everyone declared, "Nan will be missed!"
Tom took his wife to 'Lisbuthtown' to stay,
And here they sought life's joys that do persist.

---

* The Richard Berry cabin at Beechland, Washington County, Kentucky, was later moved to Harrodsburg and enshrined in a specially designed brick church housing.

† In Springfield, Kentucky.

§ *See Addendum Note 54* for list of attendants at this gala wedding which stopped a court of justice for a day, descriptions of its "infare" and Tom and Nancy, and facsimiles of its marriage bond and of its marriage return made out by one of the then best known clergymen in that part of Kentucky.

TOM LINCOLN AN APPRENTICE
1806-1808

Tom had a home* in "E-town"† then until
His short apprenticeship with Hanks was done.
When he had mastered woodcraft's art and won
Foundations for life's work by constant drill,
He wrought with aptitude and artist's skill.
Then Joe put him upon his own to run
The risk of competition, best to shun
In little towns, and counted on Tom's will.

Tom mused: "I'll make some pieces now and then
For Joe, if he has more than he kin do.
I'm sure to git most of his coffin trade,
For Joe has always said that if and when
His art must sink into the ground he's through!
But since men die, their coffins must be made!"

---

* Carl Sandburg says their cabin was near the courthouse.

† "E-town," as Elizabethtown was called, boasted among its residences a three-story frame and Major Helm's two-story brick, a brick courthouse; a doctor, several lawyers, a shoemaker, a tailor, three or four gunsmiths and blacksmiths; a distillery, a tannery, a brick yard, and a school, whose teacher was also a preacher and maker of chairs; but it seems that Joseph Hanks was the only full-time carpenter and cabinetmaker.[55]

See location on *map,* p. 68, this volume.

ANTICIPATION

The happy days flew by like birds a-wing.
Then joyous birth of their first child laid claim
To thought and pride, and Sarah was her name.*
Tom likely made some needed woodcraft thing,†
A cradle or a rocker, which would bring
More comfort to the home; while Nancy's fame
In household arts had set their hearts aflame
With love that glowed through life's awakening.

For when the nights came down and Tom was there,
Her cup was filled with sweet content, to chime
With faith as years sped by and she could share
"Till death do part." One night, in tones sublime,
She told him all, and Tom, with yearning's flair
Cried, "Nan, I hope hit is a boy this time!"

---

* Sarah Lincoln was born in February, 1807. She is said to have been named after Nancy's close friend, Sarah Mitchell Thompson, who named one of her daughters Nancy Hanks Thompson, after Nancy Hanks Lincoln.[56]

† "Being . . . a skilled carpenter, [Tom] had probably furnished their cabin in a way that made Nancy the envy of her neighbors."[57]

TOM BUYS ANOTHER FARM

The facts unearthed refute the critics' view
Which has declared the Lincoln family
Had slight ambition, thrift and energy;
A glimpse along its line proves this untrue.[58]
A trade, combined with farming, should accrue
Much thrift and well deserved prosperity;
In all their line one finds no penury.
When health was good, all work was carried through.

This Lincoln talent Tom has well revealed.
When both had learned there was expanding need
For greater income, Tom bought virgin field*
To supplement his trade and help him feed
His growing brood. Thus, by such steps, he sealed
All useless worry by one thoughtful deed.

---

* For this second farm, consisting of 348½ acres located on South Fork of Nolin Creek some 18 miles southeast of Elizabethtown, Tom paid $200 cash and assumed a small debt due a former titleholder.[59] Tom still held title to his 238-acre Mill Creek farm.

See farm locations on *map,* p. 68, this volume.

ON NOLIN CREEK
1808

"Now, Nancy, cash fo' cabinets comes slow,
Not near enough fo' four, not much fo' three.
So, Nan, I bargained for a farm that we
Kin buy near Hodgenville whar hart and doe
Run wild, an' whar our minds kin alers know
The pride of ownership's security
An' pure content." Tom smiled assuredly
At Nancy, and her eyes beamed with a glow.

"It has a cabin, small but snug," Tom said,
"A fireplace with a crane fo' cookin' things,
A hard dirt floor, no loft that we kin use,
But room below fo' table, chairs an' bed.
It stands upon a hill near bubblin' springs
Whar doves now coo their tender lyric muse."*

---

* About two and a half miles south of Hodgenville, Kentucky. This cabin is today encased in a Greek temple as a memorial to President Abraham Lincoln who was born there. The Memorial was the gift of 81,000 people, two thirds of whom gave but twenty-five cents each.[60]

CHRISTMAS EVE IN NOLIN CREEK CABIN
1808

Tom cleaned the cabin, built a roaring fire
And settled wife and child within.* The snow
Was on the ground, and wind-harps hummed a low
Refrain of "Peace on Earth." A zephyr choir
Sang melodies, as to the strum of lyre.
Tom laid a log upon the hearth; its glow
Made shadows dance a flickering tableau.
Entranced, they neither spoke, nor had desire.

The fire burned out . . . the winds began to scold.
"Come, Nancy dear, we must to bed, nor stay!"
She smiled, then spoke: "These friendly walls enfold
Us like God's arms. The springs, with mists of gray,
Foretell a blessin' that as yet untold
May visit us in this dear place some day!"

---

* There is no evidence of shiftlessness in this move of the Lincolns. Any man goes where he thinks he can get the most work and care for his family best. Hodgenville, a growing rival of Elizabethtown, was a new settlement where a woodworker and builder of houses might be in demand,[61] and, perhaps, with a growing family, Tom was beginning to feel the need of raising his own food on the land, and of giving his children proper play environment.

VISUALIZING JOY
February 11, 1809

When Nancy's pots and pans were washed and done,
She turned surprised: "W'y, Tom, what have you here?"
"I thought you'd need a cradle, Nan, my dear,
An' I have cut it fo' the little one
An' now I'm peggin' it, an' its been fun!
'Twill lighten work fo' you, an' when I'm near
I'll rock it." Nan wiped off a grateful tear.
"An', Nan, I'm hopin' still 'at its a son."

"Yes, Tom, your heart's been set upon a boy,
And for your sake I hope that's what God's planned."
Tom chuckled, drove the last peg into place
And stuffed a pillow in the cradle, coy
And shy; and then he rocked it with his hand,
As both sat visioning a newborn face.

A BLUSTERY WINTER NIGHT
February 11, 1809

The winter wind ran howling through the land
As Tom tucked blankets round young Sarah's head,
Well tousled, sleeping on a pole-built bed.
He laid a log upon the fire. Its sand
And grime he quickly brushed from off his hand,
And sat. He saw in Nancy's face the dread
Of pain that childbirth brings. "Come, dear," he said,
"Your body needs some rest—hit's life's demand."

"But, Tom, these new warm garments it will need,
That little one that God holds now unseen
From us. The baby clothes that Sarah wore
Are gone, 'cept shirts an' bibs, an' we've agreed
This one shall have its own, both fresh and clean."
Thus Nancy's needle raced to wild wind's roar.

BOYHOOD AND YOUTH
of
ABRAHAM LINCOLN

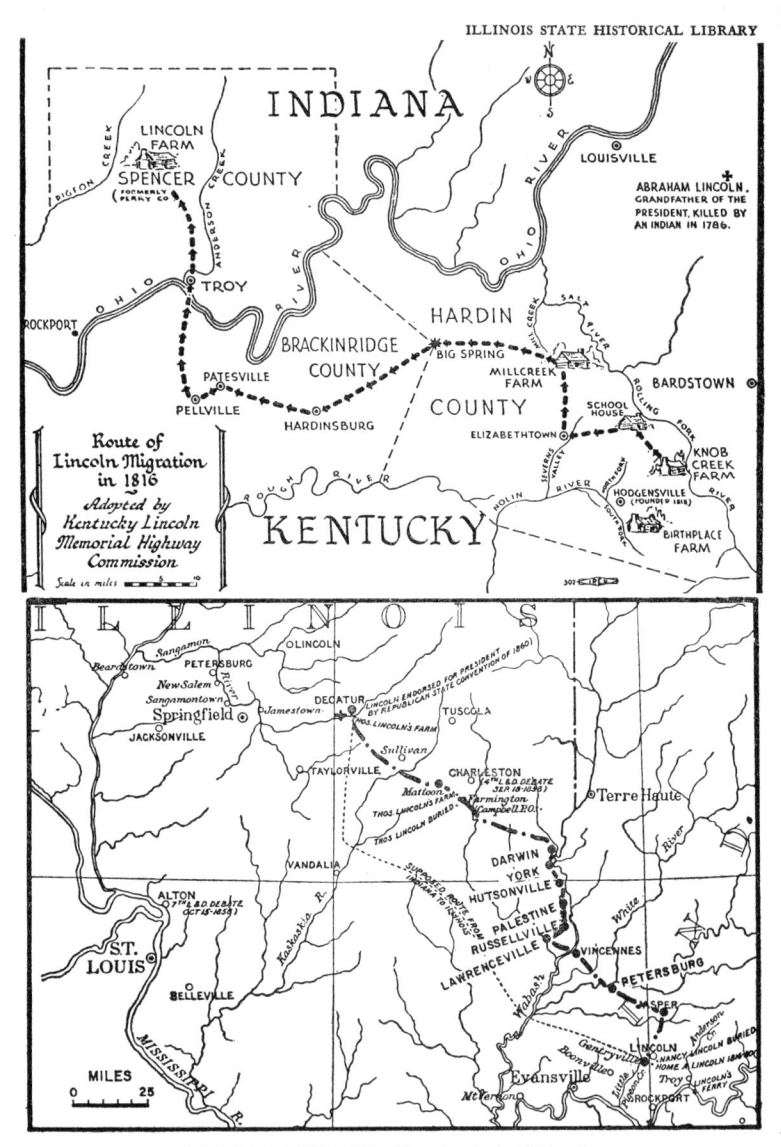

LINCOLN MIGRATIONS OF 1816 AND 1830

Upper: Map of Kentucky-Indiana showing Lincoln migration from Knob Creek, Ky., to Spencer Co., Ind. *Lower:* Map of Indiana-Illinois showing Lincoln migration from Spencer Co., Ind., to Macon Co., Ill. (The route via Vincennes has been verified by Indiana-Illinois Commissions.)

A SON IS BORN
February 12, 1809

At dawn, Tom rushed outside excitedly
And saw a neighbor passing by. "Hey! Hey!"
Tom called, "Go fetch the granny right away!*
Make haste! My Nancy's needin' her, fo' she
Is in her final throes o' misery!
Be quick! The little one is due today!
Go bring the granny on without delay!
Her house sets 'neath a whoppin' big oak tree!"

The granny came. Time dragged along. A hush
Of breathless, holy silence hung in air.
Then came . . . a baby's cry . . . a woman's joy,
And Nancy held it in her arms! A thrush
Sang low. But how could Nancy be aware
Of God's great gift to man in this small boy!

---

* Abraham Enlow was sent to bring the granny woman (midwife), who was Peggy Walters, a 20 year old young mother.[62]

HIS NAME IS ABRAHAM

Young Dennis Hanks and Nancy were akin;
Reared in Tom Sparrow's home.* A thrill of joy
Seized Dennis when he learned about the boy
That now was Nancy's care. With eager grin
He ran to view the marvel held within
Pale Nancy's arms. Then questions rose to cloy
His mind. "An' what's he called?" he asked, most coy
Yet eager. "How'd he get here? Where's he been?"

"We'll call him *Abraham*,[64] which is the same
As was his grandpap's, whom the Indians
From ambush shot and killed. It is a name
Our families have used from early clans
Throughout the centuries. I pray that fame
May come to him sometime, if God so plans!"

---

* Nancy Hanks Lincoln and Dennis Friend Hanks were first cousins, children of Lucy and Nancy Hanks, respectively, Elizabeth Hanks Sparrow's two sisters.[63] Dennis lived with Tom and Betsy Sparrow, about two miles from Tom and Nancy.

BABYHOOD

Abe toddled everywhere about the room
By grasping things he touched, until he walked.
He jabbered, spoke a word, a phrase, then talked.
When baby head sought Mammy's breast, all gloom
That hurt had caused was gone. He watched her loom
Form homespun cloth. He knew her love. Naught balked
Her fashioning his shoes from skins, well calked.
He was a woodsman's child, no pomp or plume!

He loved to hear his Mammy sing, and feel
His Pappy's steadfast arm, his sister's hand.
He watched the restless, moving leaves reveal
The azure sky and shadow-mottled land.
These child impressions lived to bless and heal
A nation torn by strife at war's demand.

THE LIEN ON TOM'S LAND

Although Tom worked both farm and trade, he knew
With prices low and markets far away,
And neighbors all exchanging work as pay
For cabinets, that dollars would be few.
There was no means but to exchange, in lieu,
Some corn and wheat or some fat hog to stay
The lien that *must be met,* until some day
He had the full amount required as due.

The Lincolns sat for hours to plan and talk,
When Abe and Sarah were asleep in bed.
"I'll get up early as I kin and walk
To Hodgenville* t' see thet one," Tom said,
"Thet holds the lien, yit he's jist sure t' balk.
Hit jist ain't fair!" Tom cried, and shook his head.

---

* Two and one-half miles from Tom's farm.

"I MUST COLLECT!"

When Nancy saw Tom coming up the lane,
She ran to meet him. "Tom, what did he say?
He will accept your terms and let you pay
The lien as folks are paying you?" Tom's pain
Hurt her. She took his hand to ease his strain
Until they reached the cabin. There, at play,
Romped little Abe and Sarah. And to stay
A tear, she bravely said, "I'll not complain!"

"Well, Nancy, seems his claim is just. 'No! No!'
He said, 'I hold a lien, you recollect,
Because Vance never paid me one red cent.
I hold first rights to that thar farm,* and so,
If you would keep it, Tom, I must expect
From you, what Vance owes me—without dissent!"

---

* David Vance had contracted to buy this farm, but had failed to meet the payments. The owner then re-sold the farm to Tom, subject to his paying the owner what Vance owed him on it. This Tom was unable to do. *See Addendum Note 65.*

THE MOVE TO KNOB CREEK

Next afternoon, returning from the mill,
Tom took young Nancy in his arms to say,
"I found a farm on old Knob Creek today,
With rose-vined cabin set beneath a hill,
Whur lilies grow with golden daffodil.
From 'E-town' hit's about eight miles away.*
I'll contract it and move us thar t' stay.
Hit's on the turnpike up t' Louisville."

Within six days the Lincolns owned the place
With rose-vined cabin that they loved so well.
Four happy years they spent among these fields
That bordered trail and pike. Here, verdant lace
Hung from the trees and shadows danced to swell
Bird's songs and blossoming that nature yields.

See farm locations on *map,* p. 68.

ABE GOES TO SCHOOL

Now little Abe was more than six when he
And Sarah went to school two miles away
Where Master Riney taught them by the day
To write and spell and sing their A B C.*
At home, by Nancy's chair, quite eagerly
They listened to her words which would portray
Some fairy stories, or new games to play,
Or tragic tales of red men's cruelty.

They learned the Bible lore of Abraham;
Young Isaac's sacrifice; of loyal Ruth;
Of Noah's ark; of Simon and the net;†
And gentle Jesus, made the Paschal Lamb.
Each story touched them with some vital truth
Of treasured lesson Abe did not forget.§

---

* While living on Knob Creek and as they could be spared from chores at home, little Abe and Sarah were sent for short periods to "blab schools" held in a dirt-floored log schoolhouse with backless benches, where all studied aloud under, first, Zachariah Riney, man of culture, manners and morals, and second, Caleb Hazel, neighbor and friend.[66]

† Luke 5:5-11.

§ How man's safest means of escape from enemies is through counseling with God; how ultimate success came to a leader of a nation who trusted God.[67]

THE LINCOLNS GO TO CHURCH

The Lincolns then attended church* when there
Were services as close as old Knob run
Among the hills. But Nancy's little son
Could not connect the parson's fiery prayer
And preaching in the church, his rant and tear
And shout, with Nancy's gospel that had won
His little heart. To him it was great fun
To mime the preacher's rant, on bench or chair.

The Puritanic faith, with all its stern
Beliefs and practices of threat and dread,
Was preached quite often to the pioneer
Whose gospel-hungry soul caused him to yearn
For gentler codes than caustic creeds thus bred.
Young Abe rebelled. His God was love, not fear!

---

* In 1816, Thomas Lincoln was immersed in Knob Creek by the Reverend William Downs, and Tom and his wife, Nancy, joined the Little Mound Church of Baptist Separatist belief. This church was also opposed to slavery.[68]

PLAYMATES

The Gollahers, who lived three miles away
From Lincoln's hut, with forests of great oaks
Between, came often, for they liked Tom's jokes;
And Abe and Austin romped and played all day.
Tom said:* "Now, Austin, ef yo' all kin stay,
I'll larn yo' how the forest talks. Run coax
Yo' Pap, an' nen yo'll know the woodland folks—
Both you an' Abe air old enough, I'd say.

Fo' ev'ry beast an' snake an' bird thet be
Has ways of 'spressin' hunger, anger, joys.
Yo' all mus' larn th' difference, yo' see,
Fo' each snake's hiss, bear's growl or wildcat's noise
Has sartin meanin's—sort o' warnin's we
Mus' know an' heed. I'll larn yo' thet, my boys!"

---

* Tom Lincoln spoke the dialect then prevalent in Kentucky, a mingling of nations and dialects.[69] Usually, however, the author of this volume has sought to merely suggest this.

ABE LEARNS THE FOREST LANGUAGE

So Austin stayed, and Tom took Abe and him
Into the woods each day for them to hear
The eagle's shriek, from which they hid in fear.
They learned the brown bear's angry growl, the grim
Wild panther's scream when lunging from a limb;
The hungry wolf's tread, soft with stealth when near;
The snake's loud rattle; furtive step of deer.
They learned to tell the anger from the whim.

And Tom taught them to track the slinking fox;
The beaver's woodcraft, watched it cut a tree;
The lynx; the woodchuck and the bison ox.
They learned to walk like red men, noiselessly,
Avoiding dry, dead leaves and loosened rocks;
And how to whistle songbirds' melody.[70]

LIFE ON THE PIKE

Life on the Pike was friendly, gladsome, strong.
No day had dawned but that someone they knew
Had stopped to chat, or gaze upon the view:
The flower-covered hills, where wild bird song
Re-echoed from the woods, and bells' ding-dong
Beat out foot-time for laggard cows in dew
That gleamed like jewels fairy wands bestrew
While woodland zephyrs wafted praise along.

Thus time crept swiftly past and Tommy came,
A second boy, whose sweetness did beguile
Them all to play once more life's joyous game,
To glorify earth-life for them a while.
But one bright dawn an angel called his name...
And little Tommy left them ... with a smile.*

---

* Tommy Lincoln was likely buried in the Little **Mound** Cemetery on Knob Creek.

CLASH OF CLASS*

Three decades passed, since Indians had killed
The pioneers. Kentucky was the land
Of promise still at emigrants' demand.
The poor, the rich, the men with slaves had filled
The place. And now another menace chilled
Men's hearts, a vicious monster took a hand.
It threatened life democracy had planned
And men had drained their strength and lives to build.

Yet slavery was not alone the lash
That stung the men whose bread was earned by sweat,
But *attitudes* the slave trade brought: the clash
Of rank! This humbling irony beset
Men's outraged pride when dubbed, "Thet po' w'ite trash,"
Because of meager holdings mired in debt!

---

* *See Addendum Note 71.*

THE FORCED DECISION
1816

"Kaintucky titles to a farm or land
Air jist not safe," Tom said. "I've bought up two
An' both air bad! So whut's th' use! I'm through!
We's leavin' this hyar state! I've got hit planned
T' live whur po' state laws cain't countermand
My rights. My payment on this farm was due
Today. It had a lien I never knew!
I sold the farm fo' cash an' boot in hand.*

A friend then told me whur t' find a claim
Across Ohio's waves, on Pigeon Creek.
Thet State is free, no Negroes or po' w'ites,
An' all men air regarded jist th' same.
Up thar's the place I think thet we should seek,
Up whur a man's a man with equal rights!"

---

* Authors differ as to what Tom received in exchange for his equity in the Knob Creek farm. He got some cash and "boot." Just what "the boot" was, authors differ, but it was likely what the claimant of the farm may have had on hand which could have been several barrels of whiskey, as some authors have stated when reporting that Tom lost all of it when his boat overturned as he was taking it to trade in Indiana. *See Addendum Note 72.*

THE MOVE TO INDIANA BEGUN

Tom went at once to stake out his farm claim
Of primal soil which lay near Pigeon Creek.*
He marked the site with stones, and went to seek
The County records,† there to sign his name,
Then walk§ the weary road back home. No game
Of sport was that one hundred miles through bleak
Morass or forest trail where prowled the sleek
Wild life. His food was nuts, each meal the same.

He made a raft to float his household goods
Upon Ohio's turbid course. He planned
To steer them straight to Thompson's Ferry hut,
And then to use a wagon through the woods
That was so dense upon this virgin land
No wagon could get through till trees were cut!

---

* Pigeon Creek runs near Gentryville, Indiana.

† Tom Lincoln's original entry can still be seen in the "Tract Book" at Rockport, Indiana.[73]

§ It is thought, Tarbell states, that Tom started by canoe, but that when it upset, he had to go the rest of the way, and return, on foot.

THE BASKET DINNER

The neighbors heard that Tom had gone to see
And choose a farm "up Indianny way,"
And so had planned on his return to pay
Their due respects to Tom's whole family
In one big dinner at the church,* to be
A neighborhood farewell. Each could assay
The virtues that had made their friendships play
A part in binding them in unity.

And when the morning worship had been read,
The feast was brought in baskets large and small,
And after grace folks talked and broke the bread,
As folks will do. Then Parson Elkins' drawl
Was heard: "Dear God, go with these friends," he said,
"And grant them love and care . . . and bless us all!"

---

* The Little Mound Baptist Church.

TOM AND NANCY VISIT IN "E-TOWN"

Though Tom and Nancy thought the move was best,
Their hearts were tried at leaving friends behind.
"We'll visit Joe[*] and folks who were so kind
To us in 'E-town,' then perhaps we'll rest
A week at Hodgenville as Mother's guest;
An' with my folks a livin' thar we'll find
A ready welcome, as the letter signed
By Mordecai has urgently expressed."

With sale[†] and packing done, they rode to Joe's.
He took them in as if they were his own;
He quit his work and took them here and there.
They ate and slept as neighbors did propose;
A warmer welcome few had ever known.
Then came good-byes, well followed by their prayer.

---

[*] Joseph Hanks of Elizabethtown, who was Nancy's uncle and to whom Tom was apprenticed to learn the cabinet trade.

[†] The sale of farm and household furnishings.

TOM'S LAST VISIT WITH HIS MOTHER
Autumn, 1816

Bathsheba lived with Mord.* They all ran out
With eager love to greet Tom's folks as they
Rode up on horses packed to move away.
With loving open arms each stood about
To welcome Tom's with laughter and with shout,
And for a week they ate and talked. Each day
Tom told them of his farm, its wooded lay ...
The settlers there; and wild beasts he must rout.

Each of Tom's sisters and his brother Joe†
Had Tom's to dine, with kindred chivalry,
Till time ran by and Tom said, *"We must go!"*
In tears, they said good-bye; and tenderly
Tom drew his mother close! None there could know
This parting was for them—eternity.

---

* Mordecai, Tom's oldest brother, who had married Mary Mudd.

† Josiah, Tom's other brother, who married Catherine Barlow, and the two sisters, Mary, the older who had married Ralph Crume, and Nancy, who had married William Brumfield, were living nearby.

THE LINCOLNS LEAVE KENTUCKY

"Now, Nancy, you an' Sarah ride old Dode,
An' Abe an' me kin ride the little bay.
In fact, I 'spect I'll walk some ev'ry day,
Fo' beddin', cookin' things, with Abe's, a load
Fo' one small horse to tote on trail and road."
Tom paused, "W'y, Nancy, would yo' ruther stay?"
"No! No!" she gasped, and brushed a tear away.
"Its hard to leave the folks we've loved and knowed."

Tom gulped, and seizing horse strap, walked ahead
While Nancy's mare began to plod behind.
And thus they went until the sun had fled.
"This woods and creek," Tom called, "is best we'll find
Fo' makin' camp. We'll stop and eat and bed."
Tom built a fire. Then, night and sleep entwined.

ENROUTE TO INDIANA*
Autumn, 1816

The hours were long from morn to set of sun,
And Nancy, tired of riding, begged to walk
And lead the bay at times, while Tom would stalk
The furtive game. The children had their fun
By evening fires, where they could romp and run
While Tom and Nancy passed the time in talk.
Then, lulled to sleep by woodland sounds and squawk
Of flying geese, all dwelt where dreams were spun.

Young Abe, not eight, enjoyed the autumn hues;
The rolling, wide Ohio made him stare;
The ferryboat filled him with wonderment.
They rode where woodland colors danced revues;
Abe drank it in, the beauty pulsing there
In hymns of color praise and woodland scent.

---

* *See map* on p. 68, this volume.

THE HALF-FACE CAMP
Autumn, 1816

"Now, wife," Tom said, "they ain't a cabin here,
Jist miles and miles of wilderness you'll see.
So, with th' winter comin' on, we'll be
Well off t' build a half-face camp,* and near
A fire t' warm th' open side an' clear
Off prowlin' beasts. I'll cut a spot whar we
Kin build a one-room cabin, sartinly
Afore th' winter of th' comin' year."

They all helped Tom to build the camp, where they
Were safe inside when snows began to cling.
Tom worked with axe and rifle every day
To clean a garden spot, shoot game on wing,
Split needed wood to burn, and seek to stay—
With venison—their constant hungering.

---

* "Many mournful pictures have been drawn of this first shelter of the Lincolns in Indiana, but the half-face camp was like the sod house of the prairie, the shack of the mining town, and quite as good as either." For perhaps the most authentic description of the Lincoln half-face camp, *see Addendum Note 74.*

ABE LEARNS TO USE THE AXE

Tom's work was strenuous on Pigeon Creek;
And since young Abe was strong as boys of ten,
Tom taught him in his urgent need of men
To use the maul and axe to clear the bleak,
Dense woods around their half-face camp. In meek
Obedience, Abe helped in woodland glen;
And routed cat and wolf each time again.
Soon Abe developed a superb physique.

In later years, Abe often said: "My 'Pap
Taught me t' work, but not t' love it,' so
I've known small ease in work I've had t' do.
Pap told me of my Grandpap's fate, the rap
He had t' bear in consequence: t' go
Through life denied the father-love I knew."

THE LINCOLNS FIND FOOD

The Lincolns, like all pioneers, found food
About them everywhere. One day they killed
A turkey and the next a deer, or thrilled
At sight of pigeon pie, or squirrel, stewed;
Perhaps a rabbit fried from numerous brood,
Or yellow catfish from the creek. Well-grilled,
With luscious pawpaws or persimmons chilled
And creamed, these always met the Lincolns' mood.

Wild plums and crabs, blue grapes and nuts grew here;
And bees stored honey in some hollow tree,
For them to find! A primal spot God blessed
And held reserved for man to claim and clear
For corn and wheat, man's only need to be
Yet met, when cabin stood on hillside crest!

PIONEER COURAGE

The strange environment was felt by all;
The deep primeval woods shut them away
From humankind for many months. Each day
The forest gloom had hung its moody pall
Of loneliness. They missed the rose-clad wall,
The hut, the traveled pike where friendships' sway
Was known to them, that now left only gay
And happy hours which memories enthrall.

Not many settlers here, and far apart!
Much land was yet unclaimed—the grant was new,
Its primal state untouched by white man's hand.
It boasted neither church nor school where heart
And mind are trained. All felt this lack and few
Of them could doubt such cultural demand.

THE HOME WAS CHURCH AND SCHOOL

Years passed. More settlers had arrived to share
The land. The Lincoln dream, as neighbors knew,
Was of the need for church, and schoolhouse, too.
These pioneers were men who felt life's dare
And met on Sundays in some home for prayer.
The parsons and the teachers were so few:
Itinerants who stopped while passing through,
Then hurried on to lighten others' care!

And Nancy felt her children must go lame
Through life, unless their home was made a school.
Abe worked all day with maul and axe. At night,
Before the winter fire, she had first claim
Of his short time, and read from books.* Her rule
Was this: "Now I have read, you must recite!"

---

* Nancy likely read from the Bible, *Pilgrim's Progress* and *Robinson Crusoe*.

THE MEMORY TEST

Because they had to memorize, she made
The children listen to her every word,
And many times they were most deeply stirred.
And thus they learned to think and feel, strong aid
To memory. Her son received well-laid
Foundations thus for clarity unblurred—
In writing and in speech, no better heard
In any college Abe might have assayed.*

Tom sat and smoked, then turning said, "Let me
Tell them how men have suffered much to live
As patriots and not as slaves." Tom's art
Held both the children's thoughts attentively.
These oral teachings were most formative[75]
In building strength of mind and depth of heart.

---

* Lincoln had a photographic memory.

TOM CONTINUES HIS STORY

The children asked, "Pap, is your story true?"
Tom nodded, "Yes, now bring yo' stools up here
An' I will tell about *my time o' fear.*
One day while Pap was pullin' weeds from new
Broke ground, an Indian crept up and slew
Him as he worked. I saw him fall—so near
I was to him! And then a shot rang clear
From brother's gun, who guarded fields in view.

Pap had set him with rifle in th' lof'
An' while th' Indian was draggin' me,
To save my life my brother shot him dead.
My younger brother, hearin' shots, ran off
T' rouse th' fort. Men came an' set us free.
'Lad, you've avenged yo' Pappy's life,' they said."*

---

* Tom must have told this story very well, indeed, both because he had actually witnessed the event himself, and because his son, Abraham, is known to have later recorded that it was the legend most vividly impressed upon his memory.[76]

THE BURIAL OF CAPTAIN LINCOLN

"An' nen what happened, Pap?" Abe asked. "Well, son,
Th' neighbors came from far an' near, and they
Dressed Pap in soldier clothes an' then all day
Th' flag waved over him. Pap's work was done!
All knowed Pap was a captain that had won
His rank through bravery, an' much dismay
Was felt by all, for with *him* laid away
All sensed a greater danger had begun."

Tom's eyes were sad, "Now neighbors also knew
Pap fought for them in early border fights,
An' kept them safe on their Kaintucky land
That all had purchased an' held contracts to.
But red men did not comprehend our rights,
An' hated Pap because of his brave stand."

CHARACTER BUILDING

Parental love now stored Abe's eager mind
With virtues which were sensed as vital seed.
And all ignoble thoughts that would impede
Were made to face the truths love had enshrined.
His ordered intellect took form, the kind
That people marvel at and have agreed:
His memory excelled all men. No need
Or lack of schooling made him unrefined.

Commitments from the Holy Writ's review—
A task adjudged a part of childhood's day—
Would help, through holocaust of war, imbue
The faith which carried on without dismay.
And thus Abe learned, far better than men knew,
The means that made him victor in life's fray.

ABE AND MASTER CRAWFORD
1818-1819

Two years passed by, and Andrew Crawford sought
To teach at Pigeon Creek. With girls and boys
He was a master, kind but strict. "No noise!"
He said, "and just these classes will be taught:*
Beginners and Advanced." Now Abe was caught
In the beginners' class. Such plight destroys
An eager will to learn, hence heartfelt joys
Were Abe's when Crawford said, "How well you've wrought!

My boy, your work has reached the grade and passed,
You're able now to multiply and add.
Improve your reading, learn and love it, too!
Within these books a wonder-world is massed,
If all will search and read them well. My lad,
Give life your best, life's best is meant for you!"

---

* "Spelling, reading, writing and 'ciphering to single rule of 3 no further' were taught. . . Punishment was administered by whipping or making the child wear the 'dunce cap'. . . 'Crawford . . . tried to learn us manners,' relates Nathaniel Grigsby, showing the pupils how to enter a room, the formalities of introduction and the like."[77]

A CHURCH IS BUILT

The Lincoln names—search anywhere—are found
On church books where they lived. Each Sunday morn
They met in homes* to hear some creedist warn
That all but *the* "elect" were souls hell-bound.
Such biased faith some preachers tried to pound
Within the avid mind by force or scorn.
Though Abe was only ten, he felt the thorn
Of prejudice their fury would resound.

His parents taught that *whosoever will*†
May come,—by choice, man gains eternal life.
They taught that God is wisdom, *love* and power;
A kind, forgiving God who longs to fill
Soul-hungering, and ease all human strife;
A present, loving Friend each day, each hour.

---

* A church was organized in 1816 and built in 1822.

† The Lincolns held a liberal view, though they worshiped with "strict or close" Baptists.

THE NEW CABIN
1817

Tom had the new log cabin almost done.
It still had windows to be cut and door
To close. Although it had but earthen floor,
It had substantial walls and roof no sun
Or rain could penetrate. His work had won
The praise of neighbors everywhere, who swore
The clay-stick chimney, broad of hearth, would pour
The heat into the room by measured ton.

There was a loft for Abe, with room to spare,
And wall-pegs to be set for him to climb.
There was a stoop and giant tree to shade
And shelter it, the answer to a prayer!
Tom's hands were full! He needed rest and time,
With grain to plant and coffins to be made.

---

* "It was a big cabin for the time, eighteen feet square, with a loft and a huge chimney. . . The location is marked today by a marble slab."[78]

THE LINCOLN LIBRARY

The Lincolns shared six worthy books.* Abe's zest
For knowledge lured him on to read each one.
From lessons which they taught, there had been spun
A growth and bent of character that blessed
Not him alone, but all mankind, when test
Of leadership had come. This woodman's son,
Amidst men's bickerings and flash of gun,
Stood for the right and offered up his best.

From these six books he gained belief in God,
A faith immovable, a love of truth,
And color for his arguments. They gave
Him courage, and by spirit's gentle prod,
A love for men, with tenderness, forsooth,
To bathe a wound and bolster up the brave.

---

* "The boyhood home of Abraham Lincoln had a library of six books,— the Bible, *Pilgrim's Progress, Aesop's Fables, Robinson Crusoe*, Weem's *Life of Washington* and a *History of the United States.*"[79]

THE LETTER

"I's got a letter, Nancy, for yo's here!
I guess hit's bringin' news, maybe?" Tom said.
And Nancy took it with a smile and read
It all, and then she brushed a happy tear.
"Yes, hit's from Paps. They're comin' up this year."*
"Well now," Tom mused, "I sure mus' get th' bed
An pegs t' reach the lof' up overhead
All done in our new house, and finished, dear.

I'll get t' work on hit this very day.
I'd like t' put the wooden door up, too,
And then we all kin move right in t' stay.
Your folks kin use this camp the autumn through,
Till we kin get their'n done. What does yo' say?"
"O, Pappy, let me help!" Abe cried, "Please do!"

---

* In the fall of 1817 they were joined by Nancy's foster parents and close neighbors in Kentucky, her uncle and aunt, Tom and Betsy Sparrow, and their other foster child, Nancy's cousin, Dennis Hanks, a lad some ten years older than Abe.[80]

REUNION

It had been but a short twelve months since they,
The Sparrow and the Lincoln families,
Had parted, yet those months seemed centuries.
Each counted hours that dragged until the day
When paths should cross again and all could pay
Their love in word or tender sympathies.
That time at last had come, and now at ease,
They talked and laughed the happy hours away.

With hopes and courage high, and love aglow,
The weeks ran on and brought much happiness
To all, for none could sense the awesome foe
That, like a specter, crept in somber dress
To snatch their loved ones from the fold—a woe
Which soon would touch their lives with loneliness.

THE MILK-SICK SCOURGE
1818

"Poor Mammy," Nancy cried. "What's wrong with you
And Pap? You's all so sick! No doctor near!*
Now, if it is contagion, it is clear
It's best that Tom an' Dennis an' my two
Should keep apart from us. I'll surely do
My best at nursin' yo' in this camp here."
And Nancy gave them both good care and cheer,
But morning brought an end of hopes she knew.

Their writhing agony had silenced talk.
Then—one long struggling gasp, and both lay dead!
It was but yesterday they learned that stock,
And humans all about, were down abed
From some strange malady no cure could balk.†
Her grief was keen—she sensed a fearful dread.

---

* It was 35 miles to the nearest doctor.

† It has been said that "Milk-Sick" resulted from cow's milk after they had eaten white Poke root, which poisoned the milk. But at that time it was thought to be perhaps an intensified form of malaria, an advanced stage of the chills, fever and ague common in that region due to the poisons which rose into the air from the rank malarious mass of water-soaked leaf mould prevalent.

MADONNA OF THE WILDWOOD
October 5, 1818

Then Nancy, who had nursed and watched beside
The beds of dear ones, gave a sigh as *she*
Turned from their graves *in milk-sick misery;*
And from her pain-wracked bed young Nancy cried:
"Dear Tom, I cannot longer here abide—
I soon must go! . . . O, children, promise me
You both will put your faith in God, for He
Will act as Counselor—He's been my Guide!"

The gentle eyes closed in their last long sleep.
The autumn music played through every leaf,
Re-echoing glad Heaven's welcome lay!
But in the hut, Abe sat alone—to weep
Close to her bed, and breathe a vow: "No grief
Shall mar my mother's counsel through life's day!"

---

* Milk-sick was deadly and rapid. Nancy was ill but seven days.

NANCY'S BURIAL

Death soothed the pain-filled face into a smile.
The children washed and dressed her form and stayed
Her braids with pins, till Tom had sawed and made
Her plain wood coffin that Abe pegged meanwhile.
They bore her through the forest temple-aisle
Just as the sun was gilding leaf and blade,
And sank her coffin while the breezes played
A requiem no sorrow could beguile.*

They heard the fall of cold, clay clods, a sound†
That roused an agony no words could tell.
They felt the need of hymns, a man of prayer,
To comfort them and consecrate the ground.
That night a single star stood sentinel
Above the grave, while in the home—despair!

---

* Neighbors were dying, and each family was burying its own dead—from fear of contagion.

† Nancy Hanks Lincoln was buried just at sunset, without a sermon or a song. The only sounds which remained were those of the evening breezes sighing through the trees, and the sobs of Tom, Dennis and the children, Abe and Sarah.

"SAINT JOHN OF THE WILDERNESS"

The months ran by. No parsons came to bless
With Christian burial the one held dear.
One day Abe said, "Pap, there is paper here.
Let's write[81] to Saint John of the Wilderness!*
That parson Mammy always liked, I guess
Because his gospel is of love—not fear!
It's lonely, Pap! I can't keep back the tear."
Tom noded—and gave Abe a warm caress.

Abe sent the letter to an elder there
At Knob Creek Church, and Parson Elkins wrote
And said, "Be with you in a month or two."
One day he came, with sermon, song and prayer,
And many Bible passages to quote,
And left the Lincolns comforted anew.†

---

* Parson David Elkins was known as "Saint John of the Wilderness."

† This memorial service for Nancy Hanks Lincoln likely included also the Sparrows, Tom and Betsy, Nancy's foster parents.

LONGINGS AND MEMORIES

Red leaves of autumn fell—and winter came,
With chill and ice and howling winds that blow;
For months the Lincolns were housed up by snow,
Then spring's jade-green fringed trees. All felt the same
Deep heartache—loneliness! It was Tom's aim
To mother them through dragging months of woe
When they longed for her form that they missed so!
These grief-filled days set memories aflame!

Each one, each day, through frost or sunny air,
Stood by her grave, felt cravings to be near
Her mortal dust; and each one breathed a prayer.
When summer dawned it brought the songbird's cheer;
They gathered woodland buds and left them there.
But in their hearts was gloom—that would not clear.

TOM SEES A NEED

The cabin never had been more awry;
Their clothes, half washed, were dingy from the soil.
Tom felt the rub. While Nancy lived, such roil
Was never seen; her will, her hands, her eye
And strength were trained to meet their needs. But try
Her best, young Sarah, only twelve, would toil
All day to wash and cook, to know but moil.*
Tom saw the need and mulled it with a sigh.

"Now, Sarah's at the age *she* should have care.
Her will is strong, but needs a mother's shield
And counseling, and ready hands to share
The efforts here. For Abe can't help, and wield
The axe and maul!" . . . Tom sat alone, aware
Of needs to which his taut heartstrings *must* yield.

---

* Drudgery.

ABSENCE

Tom sat upon his horse one winter day:
"Now, Dennis,* yo' take keer o' them," he said,
"I'm goin' 'cross th' broad Ohio. Dread
Th' long, cold ride, but feel I ought t' pay
A visit t' some old-time friends, let's say
Fo' 'bout three weeks or so. Yo' cut thet dead
Oak tree, build fence, an' keep th' stock well fed.
A little work will pass th' time away."

The days crept on, till near three weeks ran by.
Each daylight hour, Abe searched the woodland trail
Where Tom had journeyed off. He longed to bless
Tom's safe return. Fear-filled, Abe wondered why
He had not come. The night owl's hoot, and wail
Of whippoorwill, increased his loneliness.

---

* Dennis Hanks, Nancy's cousin, was now 19. He and Nancy had been reared by Thomas and Elizabeth Sparrow, so when they died Tom and Nancy had made him a member of their household. Tom felt Dennis could be trusted to care for the children while he was gone.

LONESOME CHILDREN

"It's lonesome now!" Abe moaned. "I'm lonely, too,"
Said Sarah wistfully, "wish Pap was here!
Pap's been away a month—Sometimes I fear—"
"Now, Sarah," answered Dennis, "Yo' Pap knew
I'd care fo' both o' yo's—now please don't stew.
But—I kin tell how yo'uns feels!" A tear
Coursed down *his* cheek. "I miss yo' Mammy dear—
She pledged, when my folks died, 'We've room fo' you.' "

"O, Cousin Dennis, none will ever know
How glad we are our home is yours," Abe said.
"Cause helpin' cut the old oak tree, an' build
The fence, an' helpin' Sarah cook and sew
Our buttons on an' sometimes make your bed—
We're glad you've come. It's just as Mammy willed!"

THE BIG WAGON
December, 1819

Next day the children saw a wagon, through
The trail, drive underneath a sycamore
And on until it stopped beside the door
And Tom jumped out. A woman climbed out, too,[82]
And then a boy, and girls both dressed in blue.
Tom called: "Come, chilern, hyar is one yo'll store
Reliance in. Yo's never met before.
Now, she's yo' Mammy—she'll be kind and true!"

"I'll love yo' all," she said, and beamed a smile
On them. "With my three children, we are now
A family of eight—for God to bless!"[*]
Then came much talk and hustle for a while,
Till beds and quilts were carried in. Then, how
They chatted, laughed and planned for happiness!

---

[*] Tom Lincoln and Sarah Bush Johnston were married December 2, 1819. Sarah's three children were Elizabeth, 12, who later married Dennis Hanks; Matilda, 8, later the wife of Squire Hall; and John Johnston, 5.

THE STEPMOTHER

"Now, Tom," the kind stepmother gently said,
"Since you have planned t' make a wooden floor
And cut and build and hang a good strong door
Next month, let's get that work done now, instead."
"Well—maybe thet *is* best," Tom smiled. "Our bed
Had snow on hit last night, winds blowed a roar!
I'd planned to put a window in. The four*
Of us kin finish hit, an' end th' dread."

Within three weeks the work was done and they
Were proud, indeed! And Mrs. Lincoln had
All things within both neat and clean. Each day
Some neighbor came to hear Tom's tales. How glad
Folks were to welcome Sarah there! "The way
She loves *his* children—'specially *the lad!*"†

---

* The four who did the work were Tom and Abe Lincoln, Dennis Hanks, and little John Johnston who ran errands.
† Young Abe.

INTELLECTUAL AWAKENING

"Now, Tom," said Sarah, "with no schools about
It's just too bad! Our children should be taught,
Expressly Abe.[83] He beats 'em all fo' thought
And eagerness t' learn what's in and out
Of books and humankind. I really doubt
If you quite know him, Tom, well as you ought!"
"I've larnt thet boy t' plow," said Tom, "an' caught
Him readin' thar, till I would storm an' shout."

"But he's well mannered an' polite, much more
Than mine. Oh, Tom, well—he's just different!
While all the others romp an' play an' roar,
He sets a readin' books so real intent
He pays no heed t' them, desires t' store
Up knowledge which will mark his betterment."

THE LINCOLN CREED

There is no work so hard, so difficult,
As clearing off a tract of timber land
Where trees grow big and tough and tall and stand
Close-rowed, like paling fence, where they exult,
Defying man his right to catapult
A single one from their close-tethered band.
Tom's will was firm. His calm poised way and hand,
Well trained in woodland work, soon brought result.

He cleared his wooded acres clean and grew
A crop besides each year, that met their need
For food. He burned the stumps, plowed long rows through,
And planted grain and tilled it clear of weed.
When someone died, Tom made the coffin, too,
And Abe would help. Thus came the Lincoln creed.*

---

* The Lincoln creed was: Honesty, kindness, and industry.

ABE'S SCHOOL AT FOURTEEN
1823

No teacher came to hold a school for four
Long years, then Azel Dorsey[84] was the dean.
But during all the years that passed between
The Crawford school and this, Abe read* far more
Good books than neighbors through their life would
   score.
Such thirst for knowledge had been seldom seen.
Abe liked to figure and his mind was keen
For Pike's *Arithmetic,* with rules to store.

But when the teacher held a "spelling bee,"
With all the parents there, Abe did so well
His side would always win. Each family
Would drill their little boys and girls to spell
With hopes that one could "spell Abe down," but he
Was champion—and no one could excel!

---

* From his reading Abe acquired a clarity of diction, a mastery of style, and the power of convincing argument and illustrative emphasis by fables and stories.

ABE BEGINS TO WRITE AND SPEAK
1821-1825

While clerking in the Will Jones' store, at night
Abe gleaned the papers—learned what folks pursue.
The ills of slavery and liquor brew
Caused him concern. Abe tried his hand to write[85]
Sharp thoughts on these foul themes with all the might
And power he could, so people would subdue
Both slavery and drunkenness—not rue
The day this meance will have made us fight!

As Bacon said that writing makes a man
Exact, so Abe thus gained renown and wrote
So well the papers used his script: "We'll ban
Those ills, for when we get a chance we'll vote
Them out!" And Abe had flair for verse that ran
As natural as summer clouds afloat.

HIS LAST SCHOOL
1826

The school year's climax was the final day
When all the neighbors came from far and near
With baskets filled to spread a feast, and hear
Each boy and girl stand stiffly up "to say
A piece" that each had learned to speak the way
That Swaney* told them to: "Now, speak up clear,
Use gestures and a bow, and have no fear!"
Sometimes the school would sing a folklore lay.

It was a time when there was thrilling pride
In these achievements that each one had wrought.
The neighbors praised them all, and prophesied
Their futures, too. Of Abe, they vowed they thought
He'd be an orator heard far and wide,
If he could get the schooling that he ought.†

---

* Schoolmaster Sweeney—whose name the settlers pronounced *Swaney*.

† Abe was seventeen when he attended this his last school. He walked four miles and a half each way.

ABE READS THE INDIANA STATUTES

Few books left Abe more lasting good than one
That Sheriff David Turnham loaned to him.
It was the *Indiana Statutes*,[86] brim
With history and valued rulings done
By Old Virginia, which conveyed the run
Of Northwest territory's interim—
Between the East and West. "No slaves shall dim
This state. . ." Thus was the state's prime law begun.

Abe pondered all the statutes with much thought.
He learned they were the laws for government
Of state. "Now *this,*" he said, *"we all should learn!"*
So this was Abe's first legal book. It taught
Him rights of men, and filled him with the bent
And zeal to serve his fellow man's concern.

THE PIONEER'S SON

At seventeen, Abe had acquired the height*
Of six feet, three; was known as amateur
In wrestling, lifted weights that would deter.
He cut down trees, and plowed from morn till night;
He cycled, flailed and cleaned the grain just right
To grind, yet never once did it occur
To him his life was hard.† Work was a spur
To settler boys who had desire to fight.

Abe's life was lived among those pioneers
Whose vanities were nought and wants were few.
Here, all worked hard so all could eat and share;
No paupers, no belittling frontiers.
Their thoughts were noble, pure and high. Abe knew
Life here was lived with dignity and prayer.

---

* Abe's full height was six feet, four inches; his eyes were grey, his hair black, his complexion swarthy. He had long arms and legs, and his face was sad when in repose.

† Lincoln spoke of his Indiana days as "my happy childhood days."

ABE THE HIRED MAN AND CLERK

Since Abe knew how to work, knew right from wrong,
And had a willingness most others lacked,
Tom hired him out when work at home had slacked.
He worked in fields, in woods or house, so long
As there was need. He even hummed a song
To rock some child to sleep, or clerked and packed
Supplies in Will Jones' store. And Jones had backed
Him while he read—"Hit makes Abe's mind grow
    strong."

When neighbors came to buy, they always found
Him helpful, whether they bought salt or tea.
One ventured: "Abe, I brought this book around[87]
A thinkin' maybe you could learn to be
Like him, with all your notions good and sound.
The hero in it stands for honesty."

ABE EARNS HIS FIRST DOLLAR
1828

Jim Taylor ran a ferryboat across
The old Ohio and to Abe he said,
"I'll give yo' thirty cents a day and bed."
Abe hired to him and worked nine months. No loss
Was ever charged to him, or to his boss.
"Much compensation came to me instead,"
Abe mused. From books at night, his mind was fed;
He grew in thought by sifting worth from dross.

Boats sail the wide Ohio, like a dream
Sails sleepless minds. Abe planned a needed scow,
So passengers could board or land mid-stream.
Each trip was twenty cents a load. A cow
Was first, then came two men with thankful gleam:
"A dollar,* Abe, is cheap," they called with bow.

---

* Later, as President Lincoln told a friend of this incident, he remarked: "I could scarcely credit that I, the poor boy, had earned a dollar in less than a day."[88]

ABE GOES TO NEW ORLEANS
1828

One time Jim Gentry asked, "Abe, how would you
An' Junior like t' visit ol' Orleen?"*
"I think I'd like it fine—I haven't seen
That place," Abe said. "I've hoped t' get there, too!"
Jim smiled, "We'll need a flatboat. Kin yo' hew
One out for us t' tote a load o' clean
Field produce down t' markets in between
Us here an' thar? I know you'll take hit through.

There ain't a market nearer us t'day
Than river towns, an' we have stuff t' sell.
Let's build th' flat an' pack without delay!"
A fortnight passed; the cargo loaded well
Began the trip. Abe sold it right away.
Then, at "Orleens," they rested for a spell.

---

* To a thoughtful boy like Abe, this trip to New Orleans was an education of no meager worth. The three flags which had flown over this old city, the French, the English, and now the American—and the slave markets there—he could never forget.

SARAH LINCOLN GRIGSBY'S DEATH
January 20, 1828

Before Abe left for New Orleans, death claimed
His sister Sarah in childbirth. The shock
Was hard for Abe to take. A single lock
Of hair was all he had! His joy was maimed—
So many years they had been pals! Grief flamed,
To waken memories, like tick of clock.
His anger surged, like waves against a rock,
When told, *"Neglect* by Grigsby* must be blamed."

Then, whispering began. Abe drank the dross
Of gossip's cup and felt the cruel sting
Of deep resentment, but he stood his loss
By conning happy memories to bring
Submission to endure his heavy cross—
Despite the bitterness that strove to cling.

---

* Aaron Grigsby, her husband, was accused of "neglect."

AN ANNUAL TRAGEDY
1828

When Abe returned from New Orleans Tom said,
"That milk-sick malady, I must confess,
Is ragin' here, which no one can suppress!
So folks are sufferin' an' droppin' dead
Like flies—a yearly trouble that I dread!
No one can gather corn from fields. Distress
Is ev'rywhere, with few t' serve or bless!
An' I've made coffins every day, instead.

But now you's back, I'll let yo' he'p us fight
This siege, an' as we work, yo' all kin tell
About yo' trip. I'll saw this board just right.
Now hold that end. Hit's for Jim Morgan's Bell.
Poor Jim, he's come down sick—hits jist a fright!
Some cure should rid us of this milk-sick hell!"*

---

* Milk-sickness is a painful disease with much vomiting, headache, fever and inability to retain nourishment.

THE COFFIN-MAKER

"I know Tom Lincoln, our good neighbor near,"
Liz Crawford said, "makes lovely furniture.
I need a chest of drawers. If I was sure
He'd have the time an' he'd not be too dear,
I think I'd order one. But all this year
The rage of milk-sickness, without a cure,
Has set him making coffins that endure.
He's had small time for cabinets, I fear.

He's teaching Dennis and young Abe the trade.
Abe whittles binding pegs, all smooth and neat,
And Dennis helps him saw the logs; folks say
Those boys are doing well to lend him aid
While he is clearin' land for corn and wheat.
Oh, well—he'll make my cabinet—some day!"[89]

THE MILK-SICKNESS AGAIN
1829

A year had gone. Tom spoke: "Last year, you see,
No one could git into the fields to stay
T' gather crops, for folks came in each day
T' tell us someone else had died an' we
Must make a coffin, some for charity.
Hit's awful bad. Poor Dennis stopped to say
He now had lost some stock jist right to weigh
Fo' market, from this milk-sick misery.

Hit's ragin' now, and will throughout th' fall.
We'll have no church or school. Folks are afraid
T' congregate, and worse, each one must try
To bury his own dead, dig graves an' all.
Like when your mammy died, none could give aid,
Nor could they help us put our harvest by."

PLANNING TO MOVE TO ILLINOIS
1829-1830

"Since John Hanks writ there is small poverty
In Illinois, an' thet th' soil will pay,
An' thar's no milk-sickness, we'll move th' day[90]
Spring comes. Now, Sarah, git th' family
Fixed up fo' one long ride, an' we'll git free
O' this disease. An', Abe, now yo' all stay
T' drive one oxen team along the way.
We'll top our wagons with flax canopy.

John Johnston, yo' kin fetch them pots an' stands
An' beddin' thet we'll need fo' campin' out.
Hit might take two whole weeks afore we're thar,
But once we've crossed th' Wabash to them lands
In Illinois, we'll find th' prairie route
To Sangamon by watchin' the North Star."

THE JOURNEY BEGUN
February, 1830

"So I an' Abe an' Sarah an' her three,
An' their'n, had all the packin' done by dawn
An' ready to set off fo' Sangamon.
We ate an' looked about— Abe—Whar was he?
We searched an' yelled fo' him, but Sarah she
Said, 'Tom, let's load ourselves—poor Abe's been drawn
To kneel beside his mother's grave. Wild fawn,[*]
He says, will be her only company.'"

But as they talked young Abe ran down the hill
With tear-stained cheeks, and quickly took his place
Beside the ox teams there. Abe spoke and they
Began to move, with patient plod and will,[91]
Along the trail, beneath the timber lace,
Through streams, up hills, through miles of sand and clay.[†]

---

[*] Nancy Hanks Lincoln was buried in the deer-run, and their cushioned feet ran over her grave.

[†] *See map* on p. 68, this volume.

THEY CROSS THE WABASH

The trail led on. They saw the sunlight flash
And dance on silver waves, from hillside glade.
"The banks are brimmin' full," one cried, afraid.
Another said, "T' ford that would be rash!"
Then Abe drawled, "There's a ferry here."* With lash
He drove his oxen on, "Its likely stayed
Right by the bank." He looked about, "They're made
For streams where forders are most like t' crash.

I saw them first when I's at New Orleans,
Flat boats that gets one over at small cost.
Yes, there she is! She's steamed and ready too!"
That night by campfire, they discussed the scenes,
And trails with fewest rivers to be crossed;
Then tired and worn, they slept the short night through.

---

* They crossed the Wabash above Vincennes.

ILLINOIS

Abe crunched the good black soil surprisedly,
And walked beside the patient plodding teams
In last year's grass that flashed its golden gleams
Along some trail that now had ceased to be.
Flat prairie stretched beyond where eyes could see;
The wooded hills were left behind in dreams—
One great expanse—with here and there some streams
Where oxen stopped and drank, as well as he.

At dawn the birds kept up their roundelay,
With robin, cardinal, brown thrush and wren.
And often frightened whir of quails rose high
On noisy wings. And at the close of day,
They heard the cooing prairie-chicken hen
And catbird's call from some green shrubs nearby.

THE PRAIRIES OF ILLINOIS

When they made camp, they slept beneath the skies.
A silver-crescent moon kept watchful care,
Until they woke to breathe the morning air
And see the warming sun begin to rise.
They saw small violets with purple eyes
Smile up at them—and blooming everywhere,
With bluebells, buttercups all nestling there—
A color pageant any soul would prize.

Abe brushed his brow and mused, "This good black soil
Should grow fine crops!" He scooped some up to dream
As it ran through his fingertips, "Man's bread
Is certain here, without so much hard toil—"
He munched a blade of grass, too rapt to deem
His hungry oxen needed to be fed.

AN INCIDENT

Abe's Pappy called him back to earth's hard bed,
"O, Abe, wake up, and stop that dreamin' thar;
I know the Sangamon can't be so far,
For that is what a friendly red man said!"
Abe gave the oxen feed, ate flapjack bread,
And helped his mother lift a heavy jar
Into the wagon; then he loosed the bar,
The oxen bowed their backs and pulled ahead.

Abe walked beside the ox teams, thoughtfully.
They crossed an ice-fringed creek, then barks and whines
Made Abe look back. He saw his little pup
Upon the further bank, and called, "Pup-pee!"
It ran about and barked. Abe knew fear signs,
And waded back. "Here, Mammy, pet it up!"

SPRING RAINS

"Some days," Tom said, "the wind and rain would pound,
An' thunders rolled an' lightnin' flashed all day.
We were impatient with enforced delay,
And shivered by a rain-drenched fire. We found
A roofless prairie and a soggy ground
That would have mired th' wagons but fo' hay
Of last year's grass that helped to pave th' way.
And yet, sometimes our wagons were mud-bound.

But at sich time, when we were huddled in
One leaky wagon, with so little cheer,
I would recall some story that I knew.
Although I'd told hit often, each would grin,
Perk up and listen, for they loved to hear
It all again. Sometimes Abe told one too."

THE ARRIVAL AT DECATUR
March, 1830

They travelled over rolling lands all day,
Along beside a lake, or some lone tree—
A last long rise was reached and all could see
The wooded Sangamon flow on its way.
The blue wood smoke, which rose to curl and sway,
Marked friendly huts collected neighborly,
Like women's heads when one's in misery.
Tom stopped* to ask where John Hank's home place lay.

"Hit's four miles west and north," one said. "The trail
Leads on across old Stevens' Creek a spell
An' then turns right at top of hill—not far."
Tom bought some things and traded in young quail;
Then, driving on, went slowly from the dell,
Until Hank's hut was reached, with door ajar.

---

* The Lincolns drove into Decatur from the south, likely South Main Street, into what is now known as Lincoln Square.[92]

THE WELCOME
March, 1830

The sun hung in a sky of crimson light
As Tom drew rein.* John Hanks looked up to stare—
"Wal—ef hit ain't Tom Lincoln, I'll declare!
An' so my letter fetched yo' through all right?
Wal, howdey, Tom! An', Abe, you're gainin' height
An' brawn. Good Land o' Goshen—black, thick hair,
Yo' mammy's eyes, an' smile she used t' wear!"
He took each hand and pressed it long and tight.

Then, later, Tom recalled: "John cried, 'Come, all!'
But not afore his folks was grouped about
A shakin' hands with us. Hit did seem good!
My eyelids leaked, like wimen's when they bawl.
With supper through, we set the ev'nin' out
Afore th' fire, an' talked—as kindred would."

---

* At the home of John Hanks, Hickory Point, four miles northwest of Decatur, Illinois.

FORESHADOWINGS

That night, when all were still, Abe's thoughts could find
No rest. They leaped back to his mother's grave,
Then to the brimming Wabash seething wave.
They followed stretching prairie lands outlined
In memory, saw soaring birds designed
Against the sky, heard grunts from red men brave;
Then back where he was born, with human slave.
Each scene was photographed upon his mind.

He saw long trails beyond: "This one for me?"
He asked of one who motioned him. *"For you,"*
It said. Abe stood and stared, when suddenly
A *cross* loomed at its end! He paused, yet knew
He had no choice, for that was clear to see.
No turning back—"This path I *must* pursue!"*

---

* Lincoln seems to have visualized such prophetic imaginings as are given only to poets and to seers. His biographers have mentioned his introspective habits which grew into moods when awed by foresight and mysticism.

THE VISIT

For days they rested there on Stevens' Creek
And went about to greet the countryside.
They met some neighbors, watched one tan buck hide;
Abe bargained for some breeches, firm and sleek,
Agreed to trade them rails,* within a week.
John Hanks had boasted that his greatest pride
Was stores of corn and nuts and wild fruit dried,
Which gave them food when winter was at peak.

"Now soon," Hanks said, "we'll haul th' logs t' build
Yo' cabin down on hillside river space;
The three of yo'† kin git it mighty well
Along, or done, in 'bout a month. When silled
And walled, we'll he'p yo' raise hits roof. The place
Is wooded thick—but now, let's rest a spell."

---

* 400 rails for each yard of cloth in them.

† The three were Tom and Abe Lincoln and John Johnston. The Dennis Hanks and Levi Hall families had settled in Coles County, southwest of Charleston.

THE SANGAMON CABIN

"We stepped our one-room cabin off, anon,
To sixteen by sixteen," said Tom. "With spade
An' axe we cl'ared th' site an' got logs laid
Up high as roof—an' neighbors put hit on.
We daubed the logs an' chimbly when they'd gone.
The door space we had cut faced river glade,
An' so we hung the sawed-plank door we'd made.
Thus was our cabin built on Sangamon![93]

Now Sarah brought with her a bright pink rose,
An' she asked Abe ef he'd dig her a bed
T' put hit in, with mint an' Queen Anne's Lace
An' garden stuff—most ev'rything thet grows.
An' as th' summer passed the neighbors said,
'Them Lincoln folks has got a purty place!'"

TOM SKILLED IN CARPENTRY

"But with th' cabin built, I had to make
Us tables, chairs an' beds—I did not mind,"
Tom smiled, "for we had left sich stuff behind.
I brought a bureau just for Sarah's sake,
Her spinnin' wheel, Dutch oven for t' bake
The pone afore th' fire, our pewter kind
O' spoons; with clock an' dishes well confined
In featherbeds—so as they could not break.

But with all hands at work from morn till night,
I had them made within a month or two,
An' then, we toted in th' wagon things.
We had two beds up in the loft, in white,
And one below, with trundle bed, in blue.
I 'lowed, 'This hyar is fitten for some kings!'"

BREAKING THE PRAIRIE SOD

"Now, Abe," John said, "this farm is all sod land
An' so you'll likely need, as I've allowed,
A couple extra shares to get hit plowed.
Hit's virgin earth, the toughest sort an' brand.
Yet, when you've dropped your corn, an' hoed by hand,
With banners waving green like as they's proud,
An' later on, when stocks are bent and bowed
With weight of yaller corn, hit's simply grand!

No place in all the world I'd rather be!
Jist drop them seeds an' they'll spring up fourfold
To pay one back for all his care and toil."
Abe mused on what John said, and patiently
Broke up the sod and planted it: "Here's *gold*
That's left for willin' hands, this rich black soil!"

THE HOUSEWARMING

It was the custom of the pioneer,
When some new folk had moved in from the East,
To welcome them with contest, fun and feast,
And so spend hours in neighborly good cheer.
And since the Lincoln family was near
Of kin to Hanks, through Abe's own ma, deceased,
The interest of all was much increased
When John announced, "You all's make sure yo's here".

And so they came with baskets over-filled.
John's roasting venison on spits outside,
And coffee boiling, scented summer air!
The women served the food. Each dish was skilled
To test the cook. The men folks raced, and tried
Their strength at wrestling bouts to meet a dare.

ABE'S GIRL FRIENDS

Young Mary Warnick was a lively soul.
Abe chose her as his partner for the dance,
And while there was another beau, romance
Began. But it could never reach a goal,
For Mary's other beau sought marriage role.
Abe felt small need for girls, but took a chance
With young Jemima Hill whose luring glance
Had heart appeal that love-sick swains cajole.

Abe took her out to parties and to hear
Some wandering evangelist proclaim
God's truth. They met where some new neighbors were
To hoist a roof, or light a fire to cheer
Some needy ones with feasts of fruit and game;
But only as good pals, one would infer.

THE QUADRILLE

And when the harvest days were through and night
Came on, the young folks built a brushwood fire
Which lighted dooryard where the County Squire
Could play his fiddle for a dance. Ben Wright
Called off: "Salute your partners! Swing with might!
Now, do-se-do! Hands round and circle pyre!
Hand over hand! Now, lead her home—retire!"*
And thus the dance spun on till morning light.

When each quadrille was through, Abe would relate
Some story that convulsed them with its sly,
Keen wit. But when daybreak had come, young Kate
And George and Bet and Suse and Hezekai
And Uncle Bob danced on—their folks must wait
Till fiddlin' stopped with "Comin' Thro' the Rye!"

---

* The Arthur Murray School of Dancing in Decatur, Illinois suggested the above calls for the quadrille.

SELF-ANALYSIS

Next day, as Abe cut trees and ricked each rail,
He analyzed himself: "Why is one crude?
What makes one differ from all other brood
Of humankind?" He sought to lift a veil
That hid his weaknesses and made him quail.
In last night's dance he felt his feet intrude;
They tangled up his rhythmic step. He rued
His awkwardness that caused his pride assail.

And thus, without a teacher and few books,
Strife entered in Abe's introspective view;
His thirst to know then sent him on a quest
In search of truth. That night, in chimney nook's
And firelight's glow, he read Christ's gospel through
And found the comfort that explained his test.*

---

* 2 Timothy 2:15—"Study to show thyself approved. . ."

ABE WINS FAME AS A RAIL-SPLITTER

For weeks Abe helped Tom cut trees from his land,
And chopped and split them into rails to fence
The place. He worked long hours with diligence,
Till neighbors begged for him to lend them hand.
"I'll weave you some new shirts," one said. Abe planned
To work for her—his shirt was worn. From thence
He worked with pride and won their confidence;
Thus grew his fame, for he was in demand.

Then, Major Warnick sought Abe's valued aid:
"I like the way you work, your kind of rail;
I need three thousand, such as you have made.
So bring your axe and brawn to our Oakdale—
I'll give you what you're worth. Our timber glade
Is just across the river on this trail."*

---

* So, when he had helped his father make enough rails to fence 10 acres, Abe, with John Hanks, his cousin, did hire out to split the three thousand rails for William Warnick, the county sheriff, and he also helped split another thousand rails for two other neighbors.[94]

LINCOLN'S FIRST POLITICAL SPEECH
December, 1830

Abe hoed his field all day from early morn.
As night came slowly down John Hanks rode by:
"Say, Abe, a rally's hyar t' night an' I
Think all should go. The subject some still scorn,
But hit's the one you advocate. A thorn
As yet to some, but you have questioned: 'Why
Not use our waterways t' market rye,
An' wheat, an' apples an' our hogs an' corn?'"

They went. John said, "That speaker lacks real fire
To hold our thought. Now, here is Abe—he'd give
A better talk." Folks loudly clapped him on.
Abe stood in fear, then speech like to a lyre
Began to play. He made the subject live!
Folks praised his speech, and cheered till he was gone.[95]

AT AUTUMN'S DAWN

In woodland growths that bordered Sangamon,
Bright color-banners danced and waved. Abe could
But sense its beauty as long logs of wood
Were cut to rails and ricked. Life seemed withdrawn,
A listening hung in the air. The fawn
On cushioned feet ran by, as if they should
Not break the silent calm. Abe understood
These symphonies that played at autumn's dawn.

Wide forest glades were filled with purple gloom.
As Abe sat on a log to munch his bread,
Sun rays made moving silhouettes to loom
Like nymphs that danced across the forest bed
And lingered lovingly by some sweet bloom.
"Such beauty is not made by man!" Abe said.

THE DEEP SNOW
December-March, 1830-1831

Important factors to the pioneer
Were winds and floods and ice and snow, for few
Had ample shelter for themselves; all through
The winter, stock had none. Late in the year,
There came deep drifts of snow—for weeks! A fear
Seized all of them. As blizzards fiercely blew
The swirling snow on shrieking winds, there grew
A suffering and hungering most drear.

For stock and corn were unprotected there:
Sharp hoofs of doe and cattle broke the crust
And stood mired deep for starving wolves to share.
The Lincoln corn, icebound in fields, was just
Beyond their reach, yet hunger urged them dare
Divide the food they had—without distrust!

THE NINE-WEEKS' BLIZZARD
1830-1831

For nine long weeks the freeze lay crystal white*
Upon the land. All humans suffered cold
The same as stock out in the fields. The bold
And cruel weatherman took pure delight
In records of some twelve below. The plight
The settlers shared, with food too short to hold
Them on, was dire. No meat within the fold,
They ate parched corn to ease their appetite.

Some had no corn, and some lacked wood to burn.
The Lincolns' fare was slim;[97] besides, they had
Malaria. "Life has been mighty stern,"
Tom said. "Now in the fall I was real bad,
Then came th' snows t' house us up, with turn
T' worse—Th' awfulest time since I's a lad!"

---

* Authors report that this ice-crusted, multilayer snow was as much as four feet deep on the level and fifteen where drifted, and lay over the entire countryside for some nine weeks, with high wind often sweeping and driving icy crystals before it.[96]

THE SHERIFF'S GUEST
January, 1831

One day, Abe ventured to the Sangamon.
He tried to cross the frozen ice, but it
Broke in! He struggled from the water's pit
And walked with feet and boots as wet as spawn.
The nearest house graced Sheriff Warnick's lawn.
The Sheriff* saw him, noted well his grit,
And ran to aid him—give him benefit
Of shelter and of care—and led him on.

Then, Mrs. Warnick rubbed his feet with snow†
To cure the frostbite, while Abe bore the pain.
But it was weeks before he got to go
Back over Sangamon, in sleet and rain.
Meanwhile, he browsed State Statutes—"Good to know,"
He said. "This accident has brought me gain!"

---

* William Warnick was then sheriff of Macon County.

† Mrs. Warnick alternately rubbed his feet with snow and grease many times, to take the frostbite out.

THE MELTING SNOWS AND FLOODS
February, 1831

The four-foot snow began to melt and run
Until the prairie lands were like a lake;
Then came spring storms! Tom sighed, "I thought t' take
My chance, th' first bright days o' springtime sun,
T' move down to our kin, in Coles.* Undone
Are all my dreams, fo' now, I cannot make
The trip! Weak from this ague, with hits ache,
I'll need more time to git spring work begun."

The well-known Lincoln drive was in Tom's veins,
With visualizing of the work they planned:
Locate a farm, break ground for varied grains
And farm the fields, and keep things well in hand.
At last Tom saw the waters go! Green stains
Began to carpet all the prairie land.

---

* Sarah Bush Lincoln's two daughters and their families were living in Coles County (the Dennis Hanks and the Levi Hall families). They likely helped Tom to secure a farm in the spring of this year.[98]

MARCH CAME

March brought more rains—and little sun to bless.
Tom mused: "Although I am but fifty-three,
I'm old! Them chills have wrecked my back an' knee—
An' thet long-visioned farm, part timberless,
Is likely waitin' fo' some crops t' dress
Hit up. But Abe's of age an' should go free—
Then all that's left is Sarah, John[*] an' me.
I'll miss Abe's he'p, his strength an' willin'ness.

Come, Abe, yo' sharpen up my wooden plow.
I'll load an' wait, fo' trails air wet. I'll stay
Till I kin drive right over thar—somehow!
Thet Offutt man has promised yo' good pay,
An' he's a likely waitin' fo' you now."
"Yes, Pap, I surely should be on my way."[99]

---

[*] John Johnston, Tom's stepson.

TOM'S FAREWELL

"Now, Abe, yo' run along—I must wait on
Till trails air dried an' I kin see th' track.
I'll miss yo', Abe, an' often want yo' back.
Yo's been a good boy, Abe, an' when yo's gone
I'll wish yo' all the luck thet ever shone
On any man. You'll never have a lack
For thought or word to say, nor will yo' slack
When duty calls yo' down life's road, anon.

Hain't much I's had t' give yo', Abe, my son,
'Cept larnin' yo' to work—an' how to save;
An' reverence for God, an' honesty.
But, Abe, with sich th' best of life is won.
Now, it's—good-bye! Yo's on your own— Be brave
An' put yo' trust in God. Now, go—yo's free!"

ADDENDA NOTES

These notes are included to give documentation and additional information, especially on controversial subjects.

p. 18 — n. 1 — Waldo Lincoln, *History of the Lincoln Family,* pp. 1-2, 5, quotes Daniel Cushing's entry in *The Founders of New England,* p. 77, "1633 . . . Thomas Lincoln, weaver, came from Old Hingham, [England] and settled in this [Massachusetts] Hingham," and states that Daniel was the second of the Lincoln brothers who thus came to America.

p. 19 — n. 2 — *Ibid.,* pp. 2-5, quotes Thomas Lincoln's will, with its reference to "my Brother Samuell Lincolne," and a deed in which appears, "given to . . . Samuel Lycolne by his brother Daniel Lycolne deceased. . ."

p. 19 — n. 3 — Spelled "Lincoln" by the family from Sam to Abe, many authentic records misspell the name by careless guess or mistaken pronunciation.—*Cf.,* Marion Dexter Learned, *Abraham Lincoln, An American Migration,* chap. 8, "The Forms of the Name Lincoln," pp. 130-134; and William E. Barton, *The Life of Abraham Lincoln,* Vol. I, p. 23.

p. 20 — n. 4 — Waldo Lincoln, *Lincoln Family,* pp. 5-6, again quotes Cushing, *ibid.,* "1637 . . . Samuel Lincoln came from Old Hingham and settled at new Hingham," and John-Camden Hotten, *The Original List,* stating that one "Samuell: Lincorne: aged 18," a weaver's apprentice of Frances Lawes, sailed from England on April 8, 1637 and arrived at Boston, June 20, 1637.

p. 20 — n. 5 — Ida M. Tarbell, *In the Footsteps of the Lincolns,* pp. 1, 14. (A facsimile of this death notation in Daniel Cushing's Account Book may be seen, *ibid.,* facing p. 14.)

p. 21 — n. 6 — *Ibid.,* p. 14.

p. 22 — n. 7 — Waldo Lincoln, *Lincoln Family,* pp. 5-6, states that Dan had died April 3, 1644, and that *Suffolk County Deeds,* Vol. I, fol. 104, records Sam's well-located expanding 2-5-acre homestead which he purchased May 3, 1649, likely about the time of his marriage to Martha.

p. 22 — n. 8 — *Ibid.,* p. 21; and pp. 15, 20 and 22 state that Mordecai, son of Sam and Martha of Hingham, was born June 14, 1657 and died November 28, 1727; that he met Sarah Jones at Hull while learning the blacksmith trade; and that their young Mordecai was born April 24, 1686, and their Abraham, January 13, 1688-9.

p. 22 — n. 9 — Tarbell, *Footsteps of Lincolns,* pp. 21-23. Unlike most other early American ironmasters, Mordecai the elder smelted his own iron as well as then forging it into skillets, pots, andirons, tongs, nails, bolts and hinges. He also devised a clever triple use of the same water through a series of dams, one by each of his two mills and his trip-hammer forge; and he built his hip-roofed house on Cohasset Hill overlooking his iron works and mills, the marshes and Gulf where Bound Brook emptied.—*Ibid.*

p. 23 — n. 10 — *Located* on lovely North Scituate promontory, which at the mouth of Bound Brook juts out into the Gulf across and perhaps two miles down stream from the now gone hip-roofed house Mordecai had years before built for Sarah on Cohasset side, this *new and spacious house* of Mordecai, *successful businessman of prominence,* is a most satisfying and attractive two-story house of staunch New England design: gable roof, center entry, winding stars, oak-raftered kitchen, huge fireplace, central chimney.—*Ibid.,* p. 23.

p. 24 — n. 11 — *Ibid.,* pp. 31-32, and Waldo Lincoln, *Lincoln Family,* p. 45. Waldo Lincoln, *ibid.,* also states that Mordecai Jr. bought 400 acres of Buckhorn Manor land in 1720 and 100 more in 1726.

Addenda Notes

p. 25 — n. 12 — Waldo Lincoln, *Lincoln Family,* p. 49.

p. 25 — n. 13 — From *ibid.,* pp. 111 and 222, and Tarbell, *Footsteps of Lincolns,* p. 40, we learn that Mary's son, Mordecai, served as a Revolutionary army quartermaster; her Abraham, prominent in deliberations of State, was chosen to make the address to Washington in Philadelphia at the war's close; and her Thomas' son, Captain Hananiah Lincoln, fought under Washington at the battle of Brandywine.

p. 26 — n. 14 — Learned, *Lincoln Migration,* pp. 21-27, and J. Henry Lea and J. R. Hutchinson, *The Ancestry of Abraham Lincoln,* p. 70, state that deeds and tax lists show Mordecai Jr. as "of the County of Chester in the Prov'ce of Pensilvania" by 1720. Here he was a partner in an iron works, "appointed viewer of Tulpehocken road from Schuykill River to Oley," Justice of the Peace, and by 1730 owner of 303 acres of land in Exeter, Berks county.

p. 26 — n. 15 — Tarbell, *Footsteps of Lincolns,* pp. 37-38.

p. 27 — n. 16 — D. H. Montgomery, *The Leading Facts of American History,* pp. 154-155.

p. 28 — n. 17 — *Ibid.,* p. 155, says Samuel Adams, "Father of the Revolution," closed the all-day public discussion with: "This meeting can do nothing more to save the country," thus signaling the further action of the "Boston Tea Party," which tradition says was arranged that night in a room behind the Edes and Gill's printing press.

p. 28 — n. 18 — Waldo Lincoln, *Lincoln Family,* pp. 164-165.

p. 29 — n. 19 — *Ibid.,* pp. 52, 111.

p. 30 — n. 20 — *Ibid.,* pp. 47, 99, 93.

p. 31 — n. 21 — Montgomery, *American History,* p. 154.

p. 32 — n. 22 — Barton, *Life of Lincoln,* Vol. I, p. 22.

p. 33 — n. 23 — Tarbell, *Footsteps of Lincolns,* pp. 43, 50-51.

p. 34 — n. 24 — Waldo Lincoln, *Lincoln Family,* pp. 160, 278, 287.

p. 35 — n. 25 — Lea and Hutchinson, *Ancestry of Lincoln*, p. 110.

p. 35 — n. 26 — Barton, *Life of Lincoln*, Vol. I, p. 35.

p. 35 — n. 27 — Lea and Hutchinson, *Ancestry of Lincoln* p. 185.

p. 36 — n. 28 — Waldo Lincoln, *Lincoln Family*, p. 193.

p. 36 — n. 29 — Charles H. Coleman, "Lincoln's Lincoln Grandmother," *Journal of the Illinois State Historical Society*, spring, 1959, p. 72, and Robert L. Kincaid, *The Wilderness Road*, pp. 188-191.

"The Lincoln party followed the Valley Road southwest from Linville Creek, going through Harrisonburg, Staunton, Botetourt Courthouse, Fort Chriswell, Washington Courthouse, and on to the Block House, where roads from Virginia and North Carolina joined [and thence] over the Wilderness Road . . . entered Kentucky at Cumberland Gap and proceeded northwesterly toward Fort Nelson (Louisville)," first passing near Green River lick, then Floyd's Fork of Salt River.—Coleman, "Lincoln's Lincoln Grandmother," *Journal of I.S.H.S.*, spring, 1959, p. 73.

p. 37 — n. 30 — Ida M. Tarbell, *The Life of Abraham Lincoln*, Vol. I, p. 4.

p. 38 — n. 31 — Albert J. Beveridge, *Abraham Lincoln, 1809-1858*, Vol. I, pp. 9-10. Coleman, *op. cit.*, pp. 69-70, says: "Following the purchase of these warrants in March, 1780, Abraham departed for Kentucky on a trip to locate the land the warrants entitled him to select. He remained in Kentucky for about a year. . ."

Furthermore, Dr. Coleman, in a letter to the author, says: "Bathsheba did not accompany Abraham on his landlocating trip to Kentucky in 1780. The family moved to Kentucky in 1782. . . They first settled on his Green River farm. . . After about two years they moved to the Floyd's Creek farm near Hughes Station." No doubt they looked forward to the

Station's greater protection from the Indians, after having "proved" their Green River land while living in an isolated cabin far from any fort.

p. 38 — n. 32 — Tarbell, *Footsteps of Lincolns,* p. 63; and Coleman, *op. cit.,* p. 78.

p. 39 — n. 33 — Louis A. Warren, *Lincoln's Parentage and Childhood,* p. 11.

p. 40 — n. 34 — Barton, *Life of Lincoln,* Vol. I, p. 30. *Cf.* Coleman, *op. cit.,* p. 79.

p. 41 — n. 35 — *Cf.* Coleman, *op. cit.,* pp. 79-80.

p. 42 — n. 36 — Barton, *Life of Lincoln,* Vol. I, p. 33. (A copy of this subscription list bearing the name "Widow Lincoln" may be seen in William E. Barton, *The Lineage of Lincoln,* pp. 267-268.)

In addition to her desire to be with her friends in Washington county, Dr. Coleman feels Bathsheba likely chose to live in the Beech Fork community (near Springfield, Kentucky) because Hananiah Lincoln lived there. "We know that about October, 1786 . . . the family left . . . Hughes's . . . for Nelson (later Washington) County . . . where they moved in with Hananiah. . ."—Coleman, *op. cit.* pp. 81-86.

p. 43 — n. 37 — *Ibid.,* pp. 84-85. For blood relationship, *see* Waldo Lincoln, *Lincoln Family,* pp. 108-110.

Hananiah's helpful and protective concern for Abraham's widow and fatherless children may be noted in at least two instances:

First, note his sudden move in 1786. Business, land, survey and tax records show his living at or near Hughes Station from his arrival in Jefferson County early in 1782 through May 1786, when Abraham was killed. Yet "by July 25, 1786 . . . he had removed to Nelson [Washington] County . . . where he entered a record of more land" and (previously noted) "where they [Bathsheba and family] moved in with Hananiah . . . about October 1786."

Second, note his objection to pay his obligation to the estate *to its original administrator, John Caldwell,* who refused to give security, thus giving Hananiah good reason to mistrust his intentions. Later, the Court made Mordecai, eldest son of Abraham, administrator in place of Caldwell, and "Hananiah appeared as a witness *for* the estate." Moreover, he settled his obligation to the estate, and his and Abraham's son continued to be closely associated. *Cf.* Louis A. Warren, "Hananiah Lincoln in Revolution and Pioneer History," reprint from *Indiana Magazine of History,* March, 1929, pp. 31, 34. (The italics in above reference are ours.)

p. 43 — n. 38 — "Jain'ry the 17th 1783 Hannaniah Lincoln Enters 8972½ acres of Land. . ."—Lea and Hutchinson, *Ancestry of Lincoln,* p. 200.

p. 44 — n. 39 — Sterling Crowder, the author's paternal great-grandfather, fought by the side of Captain Hananiah Lincoln under Washington at the battle of Brandywine in 1777, but Lincoln left the army after this battle while Crowder remained and fought in both Germantown and Monmouth, and spent the winter of 1777-1778 at Valley Forge.

John Wear, the author's maternal great-great-grandfather, fought under Washington at Yorktown with Captain Jacob Lincoln, Captain Abraham's younger brother.

See Hamilton James Eckenrode, *List of the Revolutionary Soldiers of Virginia,* p. 358; D. A. R. Verify No. 251034.

p. 46 — n. 40 — Barton, *Lineage of Lincoln,* pp. 69-70. Mordecai likely acted in good faith, guarding the interests of his mother, sisters and brothers, until his first opportunity to make cash division of the land estate. Provision for shelter for the bereaved family meantime seems to have been taken over by Hananiah, who had possibly borrowed in such manner and amount from Abraham that even the returns from his dead cousin's land estate were diminished thereby, thus placing Bathsheba in "narrow circumstances," as President Lincoln later spoke of them.—*Ibid.,* p. 70.

— Beveridge, *Lincoln, 1809-1858,* Vol. I, pp. 11-12, notes that Virginia, by Act of October 1785, had abolished the English law of descents, thus leaving children of intestates to share equally in the estate, but notes also the status of Mordecai as "in a suit brought in 1797 by Mordecai Lincoln, *heir at law* of his father. . ."

—Coleman, "Lincoln's Lincoln Grandmother," *Journal of I.S.H.S.,* spring, 1959, p. 84, says: "The Washington County tax lists for 1796 show that Mordecai Lincoln, his father's *heir-at-law,* was assessed for 4,434 acres." (The italics in each of these last two quotes are ours.)

p. 46 — n. 41 — For a copy of the text of this deed, *see* Barton, *Lineage of Lincoln,* pp. 289-290.

p. 49 — n. 42 — *Ibid.,* pp. 152, 155-157.

p. 50 — n. 43 — *Ibid.,* p. 162. The sum of 100, 527, 530, 300, 264, 500 and 260 acres, seven purchases in all, over a period of 21 years, 1653-1674. His lands finally expanded to join those of Colonel Richard Lee, ancestor of Robert E. Lee, and progenitor of the Lee family in America. This "Thomas Hanks was [last known to be] alive and buying land in 1674. . ."—*Ibid.,* pp. 162, 199, 166; and (for copies of the seven land patents issued to Thomas Hanks, 1653-1674) *see* pp. 311-314.

But he was never seen again after the Indians' attack on the Rappahannock settlers in 1675-76, now known as Bacon's Rebellion.

p. 51 — n. 44 — *Ibid.,* pp. 168,171. "William Hanks was married and had a son and was living across the river early in 1679 . . . [This] William Hanks, almost certainly a son, and the only known son, of [progenitor] Thomas Hanks, was born in Virginia, probably in Gloucester County, not very far from 1655 . . . [He] died before February 7, 1704. . ." *Ibid.*, pp. 166, 171.

p. 52 — n. 45 — *Ibid.*, pp. 173-174. John, born apparently between 1687 and 1693 presumably in North Farnham Parish, Richmond County, Virginia, was the third son of William Sr. and Sarah Woodbridge Hanks. He married Catherine about June 1714. John died in 1740; Catherine in 1779.—*Ibid.*

p. 52 — n. 46 — *Ibid.*, 174, 207. Joseph was born December 20, 1725, in North Farnham Parish, Richmond County, Virginia, and died between January 8 and May 14, 1793. His will named his wife; five sons, Thomas, Joshua, William, Charles and Joseph; three daughters, Elizabeth, Polly and Nancy; but it omitted his eldest daughter, Lucy.—*Ibid.*, pp. 186-187.

p. 53 — n. 47 — *Ibid.*, pp. 229-230, declares that Joe's oldest son, Tom, "preceded the family to Hampshire County." By late 1782 the entire family was there. "Lucy's . . . baby was born on Mike's Run of Patterson's Creek, probably late in 1783."

p. 53 — n. 48 — *Ibid.*, pp. 340-342, 348-349, 187-188, quotes in full: (1) The mortgage of Joe's 180-acre farm on Mike's Run of Patterson's Creek in Hampshire County, Virginia (now Mineral County, West Virginia). It yielded to Joe the pitiful sum of 21 pounds and 9 shillings in depreciated Virginia script, and lost him the farm through foreclosure. (2) The contract of sale for Joe's rough 150-acre farm in Nelson County, Kentucky, on Rolling Fork of Salt River, some two miles above the mouth of Pottinger's Creek. (3) The will of Joseph Hanks Sr., whereby he assigned this Rolling Fork farm to Joseph Jr.

p. 54 — n. 49 — *Ibid.*, pp. 228, 230, 233, 365. Barton, *Life of Lincoln*, Vol. I, p. 63, says that after she married, "Lucy lived so worthily and well that every trace of scandal against her disappeared, and her children rose and her children's children's children still rise, and call her blessed. . . Let him who has done more for posterity than Lucy Hanks, cast the first stone."

(Several worthy attempts have been made by researchers to establish a qualified father and positive legitimacy of birth for Nancy Hanks Lincoln. However, after careful comparison of the evidence and interpretation presented in support of each differing theory, the author of this Trilogy regrets that she finds none more convincing than that given in the sources wherewith she has documented her position.)

p. 55 — n. 50 — (a) Barton, *Lineage of Lincoln,* p. 232. (b) Tarbell, *Footsteps of Lincolns,* pp. 73, 81; and Barton, *Lineage of Lincoln,* pp. 188-190, says that Joseph Jr. and his mother assigned their Nelson 150 acres to Joe's older brother, William, who sold it to enter 1,000 acres in Grayson County, Kentucky, of which Joe later bought 700 acres. (c) Barton, *Life of Lincoln,* Vol. I, p. 64.

p. 56 — n. 51 — *Ibid.,* we are told of Nancy's having lived with her grandparents, Joseph and Ann Hanks, until Joe's death in 1793, and with Grandmother Ann for almost another year, and after that being taken into the home of Tom and Elizabeth Sparrow when they had married in 1796. John Locke Scripps' *Life of Abraham Lincoln,* p. 10, says that Nancy, "though a ready reader, had not been taught the accomplishment of writing."

p. 57 — n. 52 — (a) Ward H. Lamon, *The Life of Abraham Lincoln,* p. 10; (b) Carl Sandburg, *Abraham Lincoln: The Prairie Years,* Vol. I, p. 14; and (c) Tarbell, *Life of Lincoln,* Vol. I, p. 6.

p. 58 — n. 53 — So suggests Louis A. Warren, "Romance of Thomas Lincoln and Nancy Hanks," *Indiana Magazine of History,* September 1934, p. 217, concluding that thus prepared Tom should deserve consideration among the countryside's best young ladies. Indeed, Warren, *Lincoln's Parentage,*

p. 45, says "two witnesses ... Josiah Lincoln and Thomas Lincoln, both ... sign their names in a good legible hand. This ... first [known] signature of Thomas Lincoln ... proves beyond any doubt that five years before he married Nancy Hanks ... he was able to write his own name."

p. 59 — n. 54 — Sessions of the Court scheduled for June 12, 1806 were postponed to permit the Judge, lawyers and litigants to be present at the wedding ceremony and festivities, it is stated with documentary evidence by Louis A. Warren, "Romance of Thomas and Nancy," *op. cit.*, pp. 213-220.

Ibid., pp. 220-222, lists likely attendants: The Reverend Jesse Head, the officiating pastor; the bride and groom. The bride's mother, Lucy Hanks Sparrow, and her husband, Henry; and the bride's aunts and uncles, Elizabeth Hanks Sparrow and Tom Sparrow (with whom Nancy lived), Polly Hanks Friend and Jesse Friend, and Nancy Hanks Hall and Levi Hall.

Richard Berry Jr. (who signed the marriage bond as Nancy's guardian) and his wife, Polly Ewing Berry; Sarah Mitchell Thompson (whom Nancy had taught to spin flax and make other readjustments after Sarah's return from years spent as a captive of Indians who had massacred her mother) and Sarah's husband, John; also other Mitchells, Berrys and Thompsons, and Hanks cousins, too numerous to name.

Probably the oldest present, and the one given a place of honor, was the Widow Bathsheba Lincoln, mother of the groom; then of course Tom's two brothers, Mordecai and Josiah, and their wives, Mary Mudd Lincoln and Caty Barlow Lincoln, respectively; Tom's two sisters, Mary and Ann, and their husbands, Ralph Crume and William Brumfield, respectively; others of many in-laws from the community's best families; neighbors, and even passers-by, such as the Dr. Christopher C. Graham to whom we are indebted for the following: (quoted in Ida M. Tarbell, *The Early Life of Abraham Lincoln,* p. 235).

"I saw Nancy Hanks Lincoln at her wedding, a fresh-looking girl, I should say over twenty. Tom was a respectable mechanic and could choose . . . I was at the infare, too . . . We had bear-meat . . . venison; wild turkey and ducks; eggs, wild and tame . . . maple sugar, swung on a string, to bite off for coffee or whisky; syrup in big gourds; peach-and-honey; a sheep that the two families barbecued whole over coals of wood burned in a pit, and covered with green boughs to keep the juices in."

Sandburg, *Prairie Years,* Vol. I, pp. 6-7, states that Tom Lincoln stood five feet, nine inches tall; weighed around 185 pounds. His build was muscular, face round, hair black, manner quiet and movement slow. He was independent, not lazy, but easily pleased. He enjoyed his church. He could sign his name and read some, but as other authors have said, "wasn't much for book larnin!"

Though memories' picture of Nancy seems to be as confused at times as that of Tom was fixed, Lamon, *Life of Lincoln,* p. 11, says she was: "A slender, symmetrical woman, of medium stature, a brunette, with dark hair, regular features, and soft, sparkling hazel eyes. . . By her family, her understanding was considered something wonderful. John Hanks [later of Decatur, Illinois] spoke reverently of her 'high and intellectual forehead,' which he considered but the proper seat of faculties like hers."

Facsimiles of the marriage bond of Thomas Lincoln and of the return of marriage of Thomas Lincoln and Nancy Hanks may be seen in Tarbell, *Life of Lincoln,* Vol. I, pp. 11-12.

p. 60 — n. 55 — Beveridge, *Lincoln, 1809-1858,* Vol. I, pp. 18-19. The population of Hardin County, in which Elizabethtown was located, was 3,653 whites and 325 slaves.—*Ibid.,* p. 13, n. 7.

p. 61 — n. 56 — Warren, *Lincoln's Parentage,* p. 63.
— n. 57 — Scripps, *Life of Lincoln,* annotation 3 on p. 8.
p. 62 — n. 58 — Tarbell, *Footsteps of Lincolns,* pp. 73-74. Warren, *Lincoln's Parentage,* pp. 56, 159, says: "There is no evidence that he found it necessary to borrow money during this period . . . he had ready money to purchase two farms . . . That he lent money to those with whom he worked we have evidence." He usually took his pay in cash rather than merchandise.
p. 62 — n. 59 — Benjamin P. Thomas, *Abraham Lincoln,* p. 7. The chief feature of this farm, and that after which it is often known, was its "sinking spring" which flowed out of a cleft of rock and disappeared within a deep basin below.—*Ibid.*
p. 63 — n. 60 — Tarbell, *Footsteps of Lincolns,* p. 95. The Memorial was planned and built by some of the finest talent in the country, with a total fund of $300,000, some $200,000 of which was received in quarters.—*Ibid.*
p. 64 — n. 61 — *Ibid.,* pp. 91-92. And Warren, *Lincoln's Parentage,* p. 165, states that "a house . . . the carpenters work of which was executed by Thomas Lincoln . . ." was referred to in *Haycraft's History of Elizabethtown* as "sound as a trout" some sixty years after it was built.
p. 69 — n. 62 — Tarbell, *Footsteps of Lincolns,* p. 93; William E. Barton, *Women that Lincoln Loved,* p. 73.
p. 70 — n. 63 — Barton, *Lineage of Lincoln,* pp. 192-193. Nancy Hanks Lincoln was the daughter of Lucy Hanks, who had later married Henry Sparrow. Dennis Hanks was the son of the Nancy Hanks who had later married Levi Hall. This was an aunt of Nancy Hanks Lincoln. Thomas and Elizabeth Sparrow had reared these two children. Charles Friend was the father of Dennis.—*Ibid.*
p. 70 — n. 64 — Warren, *Lincoln's Parentage,* p. 294. Seeing at the age of eight, his father, Captain Abraham, shot down

by the Indians, had left a deep impression upon Tom, of which Nancy was well aware. Moreover, Tarbell, *Life of Lincoln,* Vol. I, p. 14, says he "was called Abraham, after his grandfather—a name which had persisted through many preceding generations in both the Lincoln and Hanks families."

p. 73 — n. 65 — Barton, *Lineage of Lincoln,* p. 292, where also, pp. 292-295, the documents showing this fact are quoted in full.

p. 75 — n. 66 — Sandburg, *Prairie Years,* Vol. I, pp. 18-20, says Abe was seven years of age when he went to this Knob Creek School. *Cf.* Tarbell, *Footsteps of Lincolns,* pp. 105-106, which adds that both Riney and Hazel were likely better teachers than often credited, and that Caleb Hazel owned land adjoining the Tom Lincoln Knob Creek farm and was evidently a friend of the family.

According to Warren, *Lincoln's Parentage,* pp. 210-217, "Zachariah Riney bought the farm on Rolling Fork, near the mouth of Knob Creek and Pottinger's Creek on which Joseph Hanks Sr. had settled and where he died . . . Zachariah had moved to the Knob Creek community from Cartwright Creek in Washington County where he had known Thomas and Mordecai Lincoln." In a lawsuit, Riney's name is associated with those of both Joseph Sr. and Joseph Jr. Hanks and also those of William Hanks and Caleb Hazel. Riney was no stranger to either the Hanks or the Lincoln families.

In a court record, the spelling, English and penmanship of Caleb Hazel showed him to be a man of some education. Again, as a neighbor he signed, as witness, Joseph Hanks Jr.'s endorsement of deed for the farm Joe inherited from his father but sold to his brother William. Thomas Hanks was Hazel's marriage bondsman, thus showing their close association. Perhaps no other besides his mother and father influenced Lincoln more than did Riney and Hazel while he was in Kentucky.

p. 75 — n. 67 — Scripps, *Life of Lincoln,* pp. 11-12, says of Nancy's religious teaching: "It was her custom . . . to employ a portion of the day in reading the Scriptures aloud to her family. . . There are few men in public life so familiar with the Scriptures as Mr. Lincoln, while to those pious labors of his mother in his early childhood are doubtless to be attributed much of that purity of life, that elevation of moral character, that exquisite sense of justice, and that sentiment of humanity which now form distinguished traits of his character."

Such cultivation of his intuitive nature doubtless led to the development of a religious outlook which was not an objective, formal worship, but a consecrated, subjective devotion that daily demonstrated his reverence for, and faith in, God's omnipotence in the affairs of man.—For other training given Lincoln by his mother, Nancy, *see* Tarbell, *Footsteps of Lincolns,* p. 107, and Tarbell, *Life of Lincoln,* Vol. I, p. 16.

p. 76 — n. 68 — Beveridge, *Lincoln, 1809-1858,* Vol. I, p. 36. And taking note of this fact, Barton, *Lineage of Lincoln,* p. 83, points out that it was not his second wife, Sarah, but Nancy, mother of Lincoln, who first led Tom to become a church member, and that when the Pigeon Creek Baptist Church in Indiana was organized, Tom joined by letter, but his wife Sarah by "experience." Tom became quite active in this church. Later when living in Illinois they joined the Christian Church.

p. 77 — n. 69 — Beveridge, *Lincoln, 1809-1858,* Vol. I, p. 53, and Sandburg, *Prairie Years,* Vol. I, p. 19, state that Tom talked like others of his neighbors about him, and that theirs was a peculiar and distinctive dialect which had resulted from the mingling of the speech of many nations with that of the untaught and undisciplined speech of the settlers.

They said "hit" for *it*, "powerful weak" for *feeble*, "fit" for *fought* and "fitin' fo'" for *good for*, "stay a spell" for *stay a while*, "Howdey" for *How do you do*, in greeting. For *came out* they said "come outen" and for *much* or *many* they said "heep," for *bring* or *brought* they said "fetch," for *am* and *are* they said "air" and for *children* they said "young-uns" or "chilern"; *care* was "keer" and *because* was "caise," *heard* became "hearn" and *distance* was "way back yonder," *took* was "tuck" and *teach* was "larn" and *you* was "yo'" as was *your*, *where* came out as "whar" or "whur" and *there* as "thar," *clear* was "clar" and *certain* was "sartin," *can* was "kin" and *against* became "ginst" and *always* was "alers" and *Kentucky* was "Kaintuck." They often omitted or distorted final consonants and beginning syllables: *express* became "'spress" and *willing* was "willin'"; they also slurred final vowels: "Indianny" for *Indiana*, "chimbly" for *chimney*. *Cf. op. cit.*, Beveridge, pp. 53-54; Sandburg, pp. 19, 25, 39.

p. 78 — n. 70 — Augusta Stevenson, *Abraham Lincoln, Frontier Boy*, pp. 53-59.

p. 80 — n. 71 — Of their leaving Kentucky, Abraham Lincoln, himself, later said in his autobiography prepared for John Locke Scripps: "This removal was partly on account of slavery; but chiefly on account of the difficulty in land titles."—*The Collected Works of Abraham Lincoln*, (edited by Roy P. Basler, Marion Dolores Pratt, Lloyd Dunlap), Vol. IV, pp. 61-62.

Thomas Lincoln's was apparently a search for freedom from both slavery and poor land titles, each of which created clash of class. *Cf.* Sandburg, *Prairie Years*, Vol. I, p. 25.

p. 81 — n. 72 — Tarbell, *Footsteps of Lincolns*, pp. 114-117, states that Tom Lincoln's family watched him paddle down Knob Creek on his way to Indiana. On his boat he had his chest of tools, several barrels of whisky (taken in on the transfer of his farm) and some herbs for medicines, and much produce. She also tells us that, as Tom was approaching Salt Creek's entrance into the Ohio, his boat overturned and tools and all else he was carrying on the boat went to the bottom of the river, but that Tom managed to rescue them and store them with a settler named Posey who lived at Troy, promising to pick them up later when he brought his family into Indiana to make their home on Pigeon Creek. *Cf.* Beveridge, *Abraham Lincoln, 1809-1858,* Vol. I, p. 37, and Sandburg, *Prairie Years,* Vol. I, p. 30.

p. 82 — n. 73 — William E. Turner, *Trails from Hodgenville to Springfield.*

p. 88 — n. 74 — Tarbell, *Footsteps of Lincolns,* p. 120. *Ibid.,* also says that Lincoln's circuit traveling companion, Henry C. Whitney, describes the Lincoln camp as follows: It had three sides made of 14-foot logs pinned with wooden pegs to four topped and trimmed tree trunks, these to serve as corner posts. The opening between the logs on the sides were filled with mud. The fourth side was left open, facing the south and a huge stone fireplace. The fire in this fireplace was never allowed to go out in cold weather, for it not only served as a source of heat and a place to cook, but also to keep the many wild animals away. The roof was made of small poles thatched with branches, brush and dry grass. Here the Lincolns spent the winter of 1816-1817 with no ill effects.

p. 93 — n. 75 — *Ibid.,* p. 107.

p. 94 — n. 76 — *Ibid.*

p. 97 — n. 77 — Beveridge, *Lincoln, 1809-1858,* Vol. I, p. 56. Abe and his sister, Sarah, attended this school for a short time during the winter of 1818-1819. It was held in a cabin made of rude poles, with a huge fireplace, floor and seats of puncheon logs. A log was left out on one side and the hole covered with greased paper to serve as a window for light.

p. 99 — n. 78 — Tarbell, *Footsteps of Lincolns,* p. 122.

p. 100 — n. 79 — William E. Barton, *Abraham Lincoln and His Books,* p. 7. Moreover, Barton, *Life of Lincoln,* Vol. I, p. 121, states that extensive and recurrent reading of the Bible since earliest childhood became the basis of President Lincoln's pure literary style and faith in God's ways over man's. And it is here further stated that the books of his boyhood library were read and re-read by the boy Lincoln, and that they influenced him to become the man he was.

p. 101 — n. 80 — Tarbell, *Footsteps of Lincolns,* p. 123.

p. 106 — n. 81 — We are told that Lincoln, himself, authorized the statement in Scripps, *Life of Lincoln,* p. 9: "In his seventh year, Abraham . . . progressed so far as to learn to write . . . words and sentences. . . He scrawled them with charcoal, he scored them in the dust . . . in the snow—anywhere and everywhere that lines could be drawn, there he improved his capacity for writing."

M. L. Houser, in his second annotation, *ibid.,* comments as follows on Scripps' statement: "They plainly indicate . . . that he wrote readily, while he was still a child in Kentucky; that he had 'skill as a penman' as early as when he arrived in Indiana [where he acted] as 'amanuensis for the neighhood,' as is stated in a succeeding paragraph, [*ibid.,* p. 10]."

Other authors mention his skill in writing which he possessed before his mother died. He had perhaps written letters to members of his family back in Kentucky.

p. 111 — n. 82 — The new stepmother was Sarah Bush Johnston of Elizabethtown, a thirty-one-year-old widow, tall, light curly hair and pretty. She had a smile for everyone, and like a general gave directions to each one. Each had his own work do do, but no one worked harder to care for their children then did she and Tom.—*Ibid.,* p. 12. In his annotation *(ibid.)* Houser states that Sarah Bush Johnston "drove her ducks to a poor market" in her former marriage to Jailer Johnston, who was never assessed for property other than one horse, even became delinquent on his poll tax, and let Sarah's brothers pay notes they had endorsed for him. He died in 1816.

Before Tom married Sarah, he paid a number of small bills for her. She was honest and would not leave them unpaid. She was so grateful that she immediately took Tom and his children to her heart and earned Dr. Warren's acclaim of her, "The greatest stepmother in the world."

Barton, *Lineage of Lincoln*, p. 83, says Tom was "a good husband [to both Nancy and Sarah, and] paid his doctor's bills . . . paid his taxes regularly, and . . . left no unpaid debts behind him when he left Kentucky or Indiana or Decatur."

p. 113 — n. 83 — Tarbell, *Life of Lincoln*, Vol. I, p. 32.

p. 115 — n. 84 — Azel Dorsey died in 1858. His grave was recently discovered in a forgotten cemetery on Arthur Hall's farm some 20 miles west of Rushville, Illinois.

p. 116 — n. 85 — *Ibid.*, pp. 30, 34, 36, 37, state that slavery and liquor were two of the live questions under discussion in Indiana in 1821, and that one or two of Abe's essays on these subjects were published in newspapers through the influence of admiring friends. He wrote them with a pen made from a turkey-buzzard quill, and briar-root ink. If interested in Abe's verse, *see* Sandburg, *Prairie Years,* Vol. I, pp. 53-54 and 64, and Beveridge, *Lincoln, 1809-1858,* Vol. I, pp. 64-65.

p. 118 — n. 86 — This book, *The Statutes of Indiana,* contained that wonderful document, The Declaration of Independence, The Constitution of the United States, and the Act of Virginia that was passed in 1783 conveying to the United States that territory Northwest of the Ohio River, and the Ordinance of 1787 passed by Congress for the governing of this North-

Addenda Notes

west territory. And it was this Ordinance of 1787 that contained this statement: "There shall be neither slavery nor involuntary servitude in said territory." And when Indiana became a State of the Union, it included this tenet in its basic law as follows: ". . . all men are born equally free and independent [and] holding any part of the human creation in slavery, or involuntary servitude, can only originate in usurpation and tyranny."

p. 120 — n. 87 — Andrew Crawford, Abe's former school teacher had loaned him Weems' *Life of Washington*. Abe read till midnight, then he thrust the book between two logs where it was damaged by snow. Abe worked three days to pay for it, then Crawford gave him the book.—Tarbell, *Life of Lincoln,* Vol. I, p. 30. "But this book," wrote Dr. Louis Warren in a letter to the author, "was *The Life of Washington* by Ramsey."

p. 121 — n. 88 — Tarbell, *The Early Life of Abraham Lincoln,* p. 67. Anderson Creek was not more than 100 feet across where it flowed into the Ohio River. Taylor's ferry was at the mouth of Anderson Creek and ran between Cannelton, Indiana and Hawsville, Kentucky.

Abe's early training by his father, in making things of wood, enabled him to design and make the scow.

p. 125 — n. 89 — Tarbell, *Footsteps of Lincolns,* p. 132, states that this cabinet which Tom Lincoln made for Elizabeth Crawford can be seen in the Relic Room of the Rockport (Indiana) Courthouse.

p. 127 — n. 90 — Thomas, *Abraham Lincoln,* p. 19, states that "the family was frightened by another outbreak of milk-sick." And since John Hanks (Nancy's cousin) had moved from Kentucky to Illinois in 1828, he wrote Tom about the rich soil in Illinois. John Hanks settled four miles northwest of Decatur. Tom decided to sell out and move to Illinois. He sold a lot in Elizabethtown for $123.00 and his farm of 80 acres at Pigeon Creek for $125.00 and one horse.

p. 128 — n. 91 — Tarbell, *Footsteps of Lincolns,* pp. 156-157. The route covered from Gentryville, Indiana to Decatur, Illinois has been worked out by The Indiana Lincoln Highway Commission in its report to Governor Ralston, December 1916, and in Illinois by Charles M. Thompson for the Illinois State Historical Library and presented to the Illinois Legislature in 1915.

The two reports give us the following route: In Indiana, the Lincoln caravan traveled northwest through Jasper and Petersburg to Vincennes. Here they crossed the Wabash River. In Illinois, they passed through Lawrenceville, Russellville, Palestine, Hutsonville, York, Darwin, Richwoods, McCann's Ford, Paradise, Mattoon and Decatur.

p. 134 — n. 92 — *Ibid.,* p. 157.

John Hanks had come to Illinois in 1828 and had visited Tom Lincoln's family on Pigeon Creek as he was leaving Indiana. When he learned that they were coming to Decatur, he secured ten acres "down on the Sangamon River" for Tom and his family.

p. 138 — n. 93 — Mabel E. Richmond, *Centennial History of Decatur and Macon County,* states: "A good size cabin, 16 x 16 feet with puncheon floor, a loft, a smokehouse and barn were erected."

p. 145 — n. 94 — Thomas, *Abraham Lincoln,* p. 20.

p. 146 — n. 95 — Otto R. Kyle, *Abraham Lincoln in Decatur,* pp. 23-26, says: "Lincoln was not unknown in the village, for in June or July, 1830, he was called upon to make a speech at a political gathering that was considered important enough to be included in William D. Howells' 1860 campaign biography of Lincoln. . ." In his peroration, or climax of his speech, Abe eloquently pictured the future of Illinois.

Mr. Kyle tells us that in 1886 the intersection of East and West Main with that of North and South Main streets was named "Lincoln Square" in honor of Lincoln.

p. 149 — n. 96 — Thomas, *Abraham Lincoln,* pp. 20-21; Beveridge, *Lincoln, 1809-1858,* Vol. I, p. 104; Sandburg, *Prairie Years,* Vol. I, p. 107.

p. 149 — n. 97 — Kyle, *Lincoln in Decatur,* p. 32, states that late in the winter the Lincolns did have to have corn to tide them through the winter.

p. 151 — n. 98 — Tarbell, *Footsteps of Lincolns,* pp. 160-163, says that Tom Lincoln had run away from the milk-sick disease in Indiana only to run into a similar one in Illinois known as "chills and fever" or as "ague." They had not been in their home near Decatur six months until the entire family came down with it. The Renshaw General Store accounts in Decatur reveal Tom's repeated order for Peruvian bark, which when mixed with whiskey made a tonic that was used by ague patients.

Other members of the family seem to have recovered by spring, but Tom Lincoln never did fully recover. The deep snow and perhaps the severest weather conditions he had ever known, contributed to a general weakening of his body and left him unable to resist attacks. He went into Coles County, some twelve miles from Charleston, and there, after entering some land, died in 1851. He and his wife, Sarah Bush Lincoln, are buried in the Shiloh Cemetery near the church of which they were members.

p. 152 — n. 99 — John Hanks had agreed with Denton Offutt that he, John Johnston and Abraham Lincoln would take a boat-load of produce to New Orleans to sell for him. But, states Tarbell, *ibid.,* p. 162, "It was the first of March before they could get out of Macon County . . . so flooded were the prairies by the melting of the big snows. There was nothing to do but to buy a canoe and float down the Sangamon River . . . to meet Denton in Springfield."

Kyle, *Lincoln in Decatur,* p. 33, states: "Lincoln, Hanks and John Johnston started down the Sangamon in a canoe in March, 1831." But when they arrived in Springfield, Offutt had no boat so John Hanks and Abraham Lincoln made one. Thus delayed, John Hanks went only as far as St. Louis and returned to his farm to put in his crops. Lincoln and John Johnston took the load of produce on to New Orleans.

BIBLIOGRAPHY

All of the following books, pamphlets, newspaper and magazine articles have directly or indirectly influenced the author's story of Abraham Lincoln. Some have met her purpose better than others and she has used quotes from only the most authentic and convincing to document her statements, especially those of a more controversial nature.

CLASSIFYING GUIDE

The index of each volume in this Trilogy, of course, is a guide to particular topics; but the following Classifying Guide is offered as an additional aid in the selective use of this Bibliography. By using the alphabetized authors', compilers', or editors' surnames as key-words (and abreviated book or article title where necessary), this Guide affords a selective classification under each of the following twenty topic-headings:

1. *Bibliographies and Source Aids:* Thomas' *Portrait for Posterity* is recommended as the best evaluative guide through the labyrinth of often-conflicting contributions by major Lincoln biographers; while Monaghan, Angle, and Pratt give the choice bibliographies, here listed in the order of most inclusive to most selective.

2. *Periodicals and Newspapers:* Perkins, and Dumond, in their *Editorials on Secession,* afford the best over-all listing of sources in this area, while the final special section of this Bibliography lists a few of the periodicals and newspapers which give major to occasional treatment of Lincoln.

3. *Historical Backgrounds:* Adams, J. T., Hart, Montgomery, Elson, Kincaid, Buley, Eyre, Nevins, *Ordeal,* and Catton, here listed from national to sectional; to specific Lincoln.

4. *Ancestry and Migrations:* Barton, Waldo Lincoln, Tarbell, Warren, and Coleman; Baber, Briggs, Lea and Hutchinson, Learned, and Hotten.

5. *Biographies:* Howells and Scripps each wrote campaign biographies approved by Lincoln. (Lincoln's autobiography is included in Basler, et al., *Collected Works.*) Major biographical sources: Tarbell, *Life,* Barton, *Life,* Beveridge, Sandburg, Randall, J. G., *Lincoln the President,* and Thomas; Nicolay and Hay, Nicolay, Herndon (Weik, Angle, Hertz). Earlier and less dependable, except as noted in our bibliographical entry: Lamon, Arnold, Charnwood, and Holland.

6. *Chronologies:* The 4-volume series, *Day-by-Day Activities,* 1809-1861, Angle, Pratt, and Thomas, gives most complete coverage, while Pratt, *Lincoln Chronology, 1809-1865* is briefest but also very reliable. See also Flint, Coleman, and Ketchum-Catton, for Illinois, Coles County, and Civil War chronologies. All are indispensible.

7. *Environs:* Warren, *Youth,* Barton, *Books,* Tarbell, *Early Life,* Atkinson, Gore, Stevenson, Pratt, *Illinois,* Forrest, Turner, Haycraft, Kyle, Richmond, Chandler, Reep, Thomas, *New Salem,* Baringer, *Vandalia,* Angle, "Here I Have Lived," Pratt, *Springfield,* Townsend, *Home Town,* and Brooks, *Washington.*

8. *National Problems:* Arnold, Sydnor, Stampp, Randall, J. G., McLaughlin, Townsend, *Liquor,* and Angle, "Liquor."

9. *Speeches and Writings:* Basler, Pratt, Dunlap: *Collected Works,* 8 vols., should be used exclusively since it now includes all previously published collections. Mearns, and the microfilms, cover the "Lincoln Papers." Basler, *Lincoln's Speeches and Writings,* and Stern, *Life and Writings,* give supplementary comment. *See* also Robinson, Dodge, and Appleman, for Lincoln as man of letters; Angle, *Created Equal,* and Sparks, for Lincoln-Douglas debates; and Pratt, for Lincoln correspondence.

10. *Diaries and Reminiscences:* Dennett, and Russell; Chittenden, Johns, Jones, Riddle, Teillard, and Villard.

11. *Pictures and Caricatures; Bronze and Marble:* Hamilton and Ostendorf, Lorant, Meredith, Meserve and Sandburg, Ostendorf, Pratt, *Inner Circle;* Shaw, and Wilson; Bullard; Ketchum and Catton, *Picture History of Civil War.*

12. *Women Lincoln Loved:* Warren, "Romance of Tom and Nancy," Barton, Carruthers and McMurtry, Monaghan, "Rutledge Romance," Randall, R. P., "Mary Lincoln: Judgment Appealed."

13. *Family Life:* Randall, R. P., *Biography of a Marriage,* and *Sons,* Bayne, Bullard, Butler, Sandburg and Angle, *Wife and Widow,* Helm, Evans, Coleman, *Mother Who Survived Him,* Townsend, " 'Rebel' Niece," Stoddard, Hay, J., Grimsley, Kinnaird, Greenbie and Greenbie, and Brooks.

14. *Religious Life:* Barton, *Soul,* Smith, Jones, and Newton.

15. *Legal Practice:* Pratt, Whitney, Starr, *Railroads,* Woldman, Angle, Thomas, Townsend, and Zane.

16. *Politics:* Baringer, *Rise to Power,* Nevins, *Emergence,* Basler, "Rebecca Letters," Thomas, Packard, Milton, *Eve of Conflict,* Davis, Potter, Luthin, Brown, Wakefield, Fehrenbacher, and Pratt, "David Davis."

17. *Diplomacy and Statesmanship:* Baringer, *A House Dividing,* Randall, J. G., *Liberal Statesman,* and *Lincoln and the South,* and "Governance of Men"; Monaghan, Palmer, Hendrick, Williams, T. H., Pratt, F., Bemis, Hesseltine, Coulter, Ousley, and Adams, E. D.

18. *Military:* Ballard, Randall, J. G., "When War Came," Bates, Baringer, Meneely, Shannon, Adams, G. W., Greenbie, *Daughters of Mercy,* Gray, Milton, Williams, K. P., Williams, T. H., Nevins, *Pathfinder,* McClellan, Grant, Luthin, Crowder, Eisenschiml and Newman, and Freeman.

19. *Personal:* Nicolay, H., Ehrmann, Pratt, *Personal Finan-*

ces, Cuthbert, Eisenschiml, Bryan, Leech, Shutes, Starr, *Last Day*, Petersen, Angle, *Men Who Knew Him*, Kincaid, *Speed*, Pratt, "Dr. Anson Henry," Thomas, "Individuality," and Clark.
20. *Sonnetry:* Mansfield, Sharp, and Wood.

BOOKS, PAMPHLETS, ARTICLES

Adams, Ephraim Douglass: *Great Britain and the American Civil War* (2 vols.); New York: Longmans, 1925.

Adams, George Worthington: *Doctors in Blue: The Medical History of the Union Army in the Civil War;* New York: Henry Schuman, 1952.

Adams, James Truslow: *The Epic of America;* New York: Triangle Books, 1931.

Angle, Paul M.: "Abraham Lincoln: Circuit Lawyer"; *Lincoln Centennial Assoc. Papers:* pp. 19-14, Feb. 11, 1927.

——, ed.: *Abraham Lincoln by Some Men Who Knew Him;* Chicago: Americana House, 1950. (Lincoln as his Illinois friends saw him.)

——, ed.: *Created Equal;* Chicago: Univ. of Chicago Press, 1958. (The complete Lincoln-Douglass debates of 1858.)

——: *"Here I Have Lived": A History of Lincoln's Springfield 1821-1865;* Springfield, Ill.: Abraham Lincoln Assoc., 1935.

——, ed.: *Herndon's Life of Lincoln;* Cleveland: World Pub. Co., 1949. (Best edition of Herndon. History and personal recollections as originally written by Herndon and Weik, with an introduction and notes by Angle.) *See* also, Herndon; and Hertz.

——: *Lincoln, 1854-1861 Being the Day-by-Day Activities of Abraham Lincoln from January 1, 1854 to March 4, 1861* (Vol. 4); Springfield, Ill.: Abraham Lincoln Assoc., 1933. (With Vols. 1-3, *Day-by-Day Activities* covers 1809-1861.) *See* also Pratt; and Thomas.

——: "Lincoln and Liquor"; *Abraham Lincoln Assoc. Bull.,* 27:3-9, 28:3-8, June and Sept., 1932.

———: "Lincoln in the United States Courts 1858-1860"; *Abraham Lincoln Assoc. Bull.,* 8:1, 5, 6, Sept., 1927.

———: *A Shelf of Lincoln Books;* New Brunswick: Rutgers Univ. Press, 1946. (A critical, selective bibliography of Lincolniana.)

———: "Where Lincoln Practiced Law"; *Lincoln Centennial Assoc. Papers,* Feb., 1927.

———: *See* Sandburg, Carl.

Appleman, Roy Edgar, ed.: *Abraham Lincoln, From His Own Words and Contemporary Accounts;* Washington, D. C.: U. S. Dept. of Interior, National Park Service, 1942, rev. 1956.

Arnold, Isaac N.: *The History of Abraham Lincoln, and the Overthrow of Slavery;* Chicago: Clarke & Co., 1866.

———: *The Life of Abraham Lincoln;* Chicago: Jansen, McClurg, 1885. (Arnold knew Lincoln for 25 years.)

Atkinson, Eleanor: *The Boyhood of Lincoln;* New York: Doubleday, Page, 1908.

———: "Dennis Hanks' Interview with Eleanor Atkinson"; *The American Magazine,* LXV: February, 1908.

Baber, Adin: *Nancy Hanks, of Undistinguished Families;* Kansas, Ill.: published privately, 1960. (Most recent attempt to establish legitimate birth for Nancy Hanks Lincoln.) But *see* Barton's *Lineage.*

Ballard, Colin R.: *The Military Genius of Abraham Lincoln;* London: Oxford Univ. Press, 1926.

Baringer, William E.: *A House Dividing: Lincoln As President-Elect;* Springfield, Ill.: Abraham Lincoln Assoc., 1945.

———: *Lincoln's Rise to Power;* Boston: Little, Brown, 1937. (Factually reliable, spirited in style; deals with Lincoln's emergence in national politics.)

———: *Lincoln's Vandalia, A Pioneer Portrait;* New Brunswick: Rutgers Univ. Press, 1949. (Excellent.)

———: "On Enemy Soil: President Lincoln's Norfolk Campaign"; *Abraham Lincoln Quarterly,* VII, 1:4-26, March, 1952.

Barton, William E.: *Abraham Lincoln and His Books;* Chicago: M. Field & Co., 1920.

———: *The Life of Abraham Lincoln* (2 vols.); Indianapolis: Bobbs-Merrill, 1925. (First of modern school of Lincoln biographers.)

———: *The Lineage of Lincoln;* Indianapolis: Bobbs-Merrill, 1929. (Most convincing documentary proofs on Lincoln-Hanks geneology.)

———: *The Paternity of Abraham Lincoln;* New York: George H. Doran Co., 1920. (Proves Abraham Lincoln's legitimate birth as son of Thomas Lincoln and Nancy Hanks Lincoln.)

———: *The Soul of Abraham Lincoln;* New York: George H. Doran Co., 1926.

———: *The Women Lincoln Loved;* Indianapolis: Bobbs-Merrill, 1929.

Basler, Roy P., ed.: *Abraham Lincoln: His Speeches and Writings;* New York: World Pub. Co., 1946. (Edited with critical and analytical note.) *See* also Basler, et. al., *Collected Works.*

———: "The Authorship of the Rebecca Letters"; *Abraham Lincoln Quarterly,* II:2, 80-90, June, 1942.

Basler, Roy P., Pratt, Marion Dolores, and Dunlap, Lloyd, eds.: *Collected Works of Abraham Lincoln* (8 vols.); New Brunswick: Rutgers Univ. Press, for Abraham Lincoln Assoc., 1953. (All previously published letters and speeches together with many previously unpublished letters, documents and speeches, are now included here in this one source with editorial notes. Reliable.)

Bates, David H.: *Lincoln in the Telegraph Office;* New York: Century Co., 1907. (Recollections of the United States Military Telegraph Corps during the Civil War.)

Bayne, Julia Taft: *Tad Lincoln's Father;* Boston: Little, Brown, 1931.

Bemis, Samuel F., ed.: *American Secretaries of State and Their Diplomacy* (10 vols.); New York: Alfred A. Knopf, 1927-9. (*See* Temple's estimate of Seward.)

Beveridge, Albert J.: *Abraham Lincoln: 1809-1858* (2 vols.); Boston: Houghton Mifflin, 1928. (Excellent on national background, Indiana years and Lincoln personality. Old school on controversial subjects, but uses techniques of trained historians.)

Briggs, Harold E. and Ernestine B.: *Nancy Hanks Lincoln: A Frontier Portrait;* New York: Bookman Assoc., 1952.

Brooks, Noah: "Boy In the White House"; *St. Nicholas Magazine,* Nov., 1882.

——: *Washington in Lincoln's Time;* New York: Century Co., 1895. (Lincoln's visit to Hooker's Army is also treated.)

Brown, Ernest Francis: *Raymond of the Times;* New York: Norton, 1951. (Republican campaign tactics.)

Bryan, George S.: *The Great American Myth;* New York: Carrick and Evans, 1940. (Best-balanced report of the assassination.)

Buckingham, Joseph N.: *See* Pratt, Harry E.

Buley, Roscoe Carlyle: *The Old Northwest, Pioneer Period 1815-1840* (2 vols.); Indianapolis: Indiana Hist. Soc., 1950. (Charnwood attributes Lincoln's oddities of character to this background.)

Bullard, F. Lauriston: *Lincoln in Marble and Bronze;* New Brunswick: Rutgers Univ. Press, 1952.

——: *Tad and His Father;* Boston: Little, Brown, 1915.

Butler, Nicholas Murray: "Lincoln and His Son"; *Saturday Evening Post,* Feb. 11, 1939.

Carruthers, Olive, and McMurtry, R. Gerald: *Lincoln's Other Mary;* Chicago; New York: Ziff-Davis Pub. Co., 1946. (Documented fictional conversation; reliable.)

Catton, Bruce: *The Centennial History of the Civil War* (3 vols.), *The Coming Fury* (Vol. I); Garden City, N. Y.: Doubleday, 1961.

———: *The Centennial History of the Civil War* (3 vols.), *Terrible Swift Sword* (Vol. II); Garden City, N. Y.: Doubleday, 1963.

———: *Glory Road: The Bloody Route from Fredericksburg to Gettysburg;* Garden City, N. Y.: Doubleday, 1952.

———: *Mr. Lincoln's Army;* Garden City, N. Y.: Doubleday, 1951.

———: *A Stillness at Appomattox;* Garden City, N. Y.: Doubleday, 1954.

———: See Ketchum, Richard M.

Chandler, Josephine Craven: *New Salem: Early Chapter in Lincoln's Life;* Springfield, Ill.: Jr. of ISHS., 1930. (Revised Edition, reprint from *The Journal of Ill. State Hist. Soc.*, 22:4, Jan., 1930.)

Charnwood, Lord (Godfrey Rathbone Benson): *Abraham Lincoln;* New York: Henry Holt Co., 1917. (Excellent delineation of Lincoln's character and springs of action, though written before modern research.)

Chittenden, Lucius E.: *Recollections of President Lincoln and His Administration;* New York: Harper & Brothers, 1891.

Clark, Leon Pierce: *Lincoln, A Psycho-Biography;* New York; London: C. Scribner's Sons, 1933.

Coleman, Charles H.: *Abraham Lincoln and Coles County: A Chronology* (Mimeographed); Charleston: Eastern Ill. Univ., 1956. (Very helpful.)

———: "Lincoln's Lincoln Grandmother"; *Journal of Ill. State Hist. Soc.*, LII: 1, 59-90, Spring, 1959. (Indispensable.)

———: *Sarah Bush Lincoln, the Mother Who Survived Him;* Harrogate, Tenn.: Reprint from *The Lincoln Herald,* Summer, 1952. (Helpful.)

Coulter, Ellis Merton: *The Confederate States of America 1861-1865;* Baton Rouge, La.: State Univ. Press, 1950. (Describes **breakdown.**)

Crowder, J. H.: *Before and After Vicksburg;* Dayton, Ohio: The Otterbein Press, 1925. (Helpful, personal recollections of a participant from the Illinois township which had more Union enlistments than voters.)

Cuthbert, Norma B.: *Lincoln and the Baltimore Plot, 1861;* San Marino, Calif.: Huntington Library Publications, 1949. (From Pinkerton records and related papers.)

Davis, Granville D.: "Douglas and the Chicago Mob"; *American Historical Review,* April, 1949.

Dennett, Tyler: *Lincoln and the Civil War in Diaries and Letters of John Hay;* New York: Dodd Mead & Co., 1939. (Indispensable.)

Dodge, Daniel Kilham: *Abraham Lincoln, Master of Words;* New York; London: D. Appleton & Co., 1924.

Dumond, Dwight L.: *Southern Editorials on Secession;* New York: Century Co., 1931. (*See* also Perkins' *Northern Editorials*).

Dunlop, Lloyd: *See* Basler, Roy P.

Eckenrode, Hamilton James, archivist: *List of the Revolutionary Soldiers of Virginia;* Richmond: Virginia State Library, 1912.

Ehrmann, Bess V.: *Lincoln and His Neighbors;* Rockport, Ind.: Democrat Pub. Co., 1948.

Eisenschiml, Otto: *Why Was Lincoln Murdered?;* Boston: Little, Brown & Co., 1937. (*See* also Bryan, and Starr.)

Eisenschiml, Otto, and Newman, Ralph, compilers: *The American Iliad: The Epic Story of the Civil War as Narrated by Eyewitnesses and Contemporaries;* Indianapolis: Bobbs-Merrill, 1947.

Elson, Henry W.: *Side Lights on American History;* New York: Macmillan Co., 1905.

Evans, Dr. William H.: *Mrs. Abraham Lincoln;* New York: Alfred A. Knopf, 1932. (A study of her health and personality.)

Eyre, Alice: *The Frémonts and Their America* (Centennial Edition); Orange, Calif.: Fine Arts Press, 1948. *Revised edition,* Boston, Mass.: The Christopher Publishing House, 1961.

Fehrenbacher, Don E.: "The Nomination of Lincoln in 1858"; *Abraham Lincoln Quarterly,* VI: I, 24-36, March, 1950.

Flint, Margaret A.: *Chronology of Illinois History 1673-1954;* Springfield: Ill. State Hist. Library, 1955.

Forrest, Justin H.: *Lincoln and Historic Illinois;* Springfield: Public Dept. Works and Buildings, State of Illinois, 1929-1933.

Freeman, Douglas Southall: *Lee's Lieutenants: A Study in Command* (3 vols.); New York: C. Scribner's Sons, 1942-1944.

Gore, John Rogers: *The Boyhood of Abraham Lincoln;* Louisville, Ky.: Standard Print Co., 1935.

Gray, Wood: *The Hidden Civil War;* New York: Viking Press, 1942. (The story of the copperheads.)

Greenbie, Marjorie Latta (Barstow): *Lincoln's Daughters of Mercy;* New York: Putnam, 1944.

Greenbie, Sydney and Greenbie, Marjorie Barstow: *Ann Ella Carroll and Abraham Lincoln: A Biography;* Manchester, Me.: Univ. of Tampa Press, 1952.

Grant, Ulysses S.: *Personal Memoirs of U. S. Grant* (2 vols.); New York: Charles L. Webster Co., 1885.

Grimsley, Elizabeth Todd: "Six Months in the White House"; *Journal of Ill. State Hist. Soc.,* 19:43-73, Oct., 1926.

Hamilton, Charles, and Ostendorf, Lloyd: *Lincoln in Photographs: An Album of Every Known Pose;* Norman: Univ. of Oklahoma Press, 1963.

Hart, Albert Bushnell: *Essentials in American History;* New York: American Book Co., 1905.

Hay, John: "Life in the White House in the Time of Lincoln"; *Century Magazine,* Nov., 1890.

Hay, John: *See* Nicolay, John G.

Haycraft, Samuel: *History of Elizabethtown, Kentucky and its*

Surroundings; Elizabethtown: The Women's Club, 1921.

Helm, Katherine: *True Story of Mary, Wife of Lincoln;* New York; London: Harper & Brothers, 1928. (Contains the recollections of Mary Lincoln's sister Emilie, Mrs. Ben Hardin Helm, extracts from her war-time diary, memories, letters and other documents now first published by her niece Katherine Helm.)

Hendrick, Burton J.: *Lincoln's War Cabinet;* Boston: Little, Brown & Co., 1946.

Herndon, William H. and Weik, Jesse W.: *Lincoln: The True Story of a Great Life* (1 vol.); New York: D. Appleton & Co., 1889. (Written by Weik from Herndon's materials, it pictures a shiftless and lazy Tom Lincoln, the illegitamacy of Lincoln's mother, the Ann Rutledge myth. Herndon is a most controversial author.) *See* also Angle, and Hertz.

Hertz, Emanuel: *The Hidden Lincoln;* New York: Viking Press, 1938. (From the letters and papers of William H. Herndon.) *See* also Angle, and Herndon.

Hesseltine, William B.: *Lincoln and the War Governors;* New York: Alfred A. Knopf, 1948.

History of Shelby and Moultrie Counties in Illinois; Philadelphia: Brink, McDonough & Co., 1881. (*See* biographical sketch of Robert Crowder, his wife Barbara, children James H., R. Smith, and Andrew W., all characters in this Trilogy.)

Holland, Josiah G.: *Life of Abraham Lincoln;* Springfield, Mass.: G. Bill, 1866. (Mid-Victorian, interesting historically.)

Hotten, John Camden: *The Original Lists;* New York: G. A. Baker & Co., 1931. (Of persons of quality in Suffolk Co. deeds.)

Howells, William Dean: *Life of Abraham Lincoln* (Reprint); Springfield, Ill.: Abraham Lincoln Assoc., 1938. (A reprint in facsimile with marginal notes showing Lincoln's minute corrections.)

Hutchinson, J. R.: *See* Lea, J. Henry.

Inventory of the County Archives of Illinois, Illinois Historical Records Survey Project No. 70, Moultrie County (Sullivan); Chicago: Work Projects Administration, 1941.

Johns, Jane Martin: *Personal Recollections of Early Decatur;* Decatur, Ill.: Decatur Chap. DAR, 1912. (Lincoln, Oglesby, and Civil War.)

Jones, Edgar DeWitt: *Lincoln and the Preachers;* with an introduction by William H. Townsend. New York: Harper & Brothers, 1948.

Jones, T. D.: *Memories of Lincoln;* New York: Press of the Pioneers, 1934.

Ketchum, Richard M., and Catton, Bruce: *American Heritage CIVIL WAR Chronology;* New York: American Heritage Pub. Co., 1960. (Supplement to *The American Heritage Picture History of the Civil War.* Very helpful, reliable.)

——: *The American Heritage Picture History of The Civil War;* New York: American Heritage Pub. Co., 1960.

Kincaid, Robert L.: *Joshua Fry Speed: Lincoln's Most Intimate Friend;* Harrogate, Tenn.: Dept. of Lincolniana, Lincoln Memorial Univ., 1943.

——: *The Wilderness Road;* Indianapolis: Bobbs-Merrill Co., 1947. (Valuable. Describes most used passage from the East to the West.)

Kinnaird, Virginia: "Mrs. Lincoln as a White House Hostess"; *Papers in Illinois History,* pp. 64-87, 1938.

Kyle, Otto R.: *Abraham Lincoln in Decatur;* New York: Vantage Press, 1957. (Most complete and reliable discussion of the year Lincoln lived in Decatur, Illinois; includes his later Decatur court cases and details of his Decatur nomination for President. Fully documented.)

Lamon, Ward H.: *The Life of Abraham Lincoln;* Boston: James R. Osgood & Co., 1872. (Ghost written by C. F. Black from Herndon's notes; not always reliable.)

Lea, J. Henry, and Hutchinson, J. R.: *The Ancestry of Abraham Lincoln;* Boston: Houghton Mifflin Co., 1909. (Use with caution; has errors.)

Learned, Marion Dexter: *Abraham Lincoln, An American Migration;* Philadelphia: Wm. J. Campbell, 1909.

Leech, Margaret: *Reveille in Washington 1860-1865;* New York: Harper & Brothers, 1941. (Delightful reading.)

Lincoln, Waldo: *History of the Lincoln Family;* Worcester, Mass.: Commonwealth Press, 1923. (An account of the descendants of Samuel Lincoln of Hingham, Massachusetts 1637-1920. Excellent and reliable.)

Lorant, Stefan: *The Life of Abraham Lincoln;* New York: New American Library, 1955. (A short, *illustrated* biography.)

———: *LINCOLN, His Life in Photographs;* New York: Sloan & Pearce, 1941.

Luthin, Reinhard Henry: *The First Lincoln Campaign;* Cambridge, Mass.: Harvard Univ. Press, 1944. (Origins and growth of Republican Party.)

———: *Grant and His Generals;* New York: McBride Co., 1953.

McClellan, George B.: *McClellan's Own Story. . .;* New York: C. L. Webster & Co., 1887. (Indispensable. Contains enlightening letters to his wife.)

———: *"Extracts from Letters* written to my Wife during the War of the Rebellion," a notebook in McClellan's handwriting found among the McClellan Papers in the Library of Congress. (Even more revealing than the heavily edited version of these letters published in *McClellan's Own Story.* Indispensable.)

McLaughlin, Andrew C.: "Lincoln, the Constitution and Democracy"; *Abraham Lincoln Assoc. Papers,* Feb. 12, 1936.

McMurtry, R. Gerald: *See* Carruthers, Olive.

Mansfield, Margery: *Workers In Fire;* New York: Longmans, Green & Co., 1937. (A text on forms of poetry.)

Mearns, David C.: *The Lincoln Papers:* The story of the Robert Todd Lincoln Collection, with selections to July 4, 1861. Intro. by Carl Sandburg. (2 vols.) Garden City, N. Y.: Doubleday, 1948.

(Microfilms of *Robert Todd Lincoln Library of Congress Collection* are now in the Illinois State Historical Library, Springfield.)

Meneely, A. Howard: *The War Department, 1861; A Study in Mobilization and Administration;* New York: Columbia Univ. Press, 1928.

Meredith, Roy: *Mr. Lincoln's Camera Man: Mathew B. Brady;* New York: C. Scribner's Sons, 1946.

———: *Mr. Lincoln's Contemporaries: An Album of Portraits by Mathew B. Brady;* New York: C. Scribner's Sons, 1951.

Meserve, Frederick Hill, and Sandburg, Carl: *The Photographs of Abraham Lincoln;* New York: Harcourt, Brace & Co., 1944.

Milton, George Fort: *Abraham Lincoln and the Fifth Column;* New York: Vanguard Press, 1942.

———: *The Eve of Conflict: Stephen A. Douglas and the Needless War;* New York: Houghton Mifflin Co., 1934. (Sympathetic toward Douglas.)

Monaghan, Jay: *Diplomat in Carpet Slippers;* Indianapolis: Bobbs-Merrill, 1945. (Abraham Lincoln deals with foreign affairs.)

———: *Lincoln Bibliography, 1839-1939* (2 vols.) (Ill. State Hist. Lib. Collections, XXXI, XXXII); Springfield: Ill. State Hist. Lib., 1945. (Lists 3,958 books and pamphlets on Lincoln; but no periodicals.)

———: "New Light on the Lincoln-Rutledge Romance;" *Abraham Lincoln Quarterly,* III: 3, 138-145, Sept., 1944.

Montgomery, D. H.: *The Leading Facts of American History;* Boston: Ginn & Co., Publishers, 1894.

Nevins, Allan Frémont: *The Emergence of Lincoln* (2 vols.); New York: C. Scribner's Sons, 1950. (Treats Lincoln national background, debates, personalities, and the Dred Scott decision.)

———: *Frémont, Pathfinder of the West;* New York: D. Appleton-Century & Co., 1939.

———: *The Ordeal of the Union* (2 vols.); New York: C. Scribner's Sons, 1917. (A stirring portrayal of national background and party troubles.)

Newman, Ralph: *See* Eisenschiml, Otto.

Newton, Joseph Fort: "The Spiritual Life of Lincoln"; *Abraham Lincoln Assoc. Papers,* pp. 33-43, Feb. 13, 1933.

Nicolay, John G., and Hay, John: *Abraham Lincoln: A History* (10 vols.); New York: Century Co., 1890. (Written by Lincoln's secretaries who knew whereof they wrote. Reliable, except on Lincoln's early life.)

Nicolay, John G.: *A Short Life of Abraham Lincoln;* New York: Century Co., 1903. (Condensed from Nicolay and Hay's *Abraham Lincoln: A History*.)

Nicolay, Helen: *Personal Traits of Abraham Lincoln;* New York: Century Co., 1912.

Ostendorf, Lloyd: *A Picture Story of ABRAHAM LINCOLN;* New York: Lathrop Lee & Shepard Co., 1962.

———: *See* Hamilton, Charles.

Owsley, Frank L.: *King Cotton Diplomacy, Foreign Relations of the Confederate States of America;* Chicago: Univ. of Chicago Press, 1931.

Packard, Roy D.: *The Lincoln of the Thirtieth Congress;* Boston: Christopher Publishing House, 1950. (Good brief version.)

Palmer, John M.: *Washington, Lincoln, Wilson, Three War Statesmen;* Garden City, N. Y.: Doubleday, Doran & Co., 1930.

Perkins, Howard C.: *Northern Editorials on Secession;* New York: D. Appleton-Century Co., 1942. (*See* also Dumond's *Southern Editorials*.)

Petersen, William F.: *Lincoln-Douglas: The Weather as Destiny;* Baltimore, Md.: C. C. Thomas, 1943. (Includes discussion of Lincoln's changing moods.)

Potter, David M.: *Lincoln and His Party in the Secession Crisis;* New Haven, Conn.: Yale Univ. Press, 1942.

Pratt, Fletcher: *Stanton, Lincoln's Secretary of War;* New York: Norton, 1953.

Pratt, Harry E.: *Abraham Lincoln Chronology: 1809-1865;* Springfield: Ill. State Hist. Library, 1953. (Most helpful, reliable and brief.)

——: *Concerning Mr. Lincoln: In Which Abraham Lincoln is Pictured as He Appeared to Letter Writers of His Time;* Springfield, Ill.: Abraham Lincoln Assoc., 1944.

——: "David Davis 1815-1886"; *Transactions of Ill. State Hist. Soc.,* 1930, Springfield, Ill.: ISHS, 1930.

——: "Dr. Anson G. Henry, Lincoln's Physician and Friend"; *Lincoln Herald,* XLV: 317; 31-40, 1943.

——: "The Genesis of Lincoln the Lawyer"; *Abraham Lincoln Assoc. Bull.,* 57: 3-10, Sept., 1939.

Pratt, Harry E. and Buckingham, Joseph H., eds.: "Illinois, As Lincoln Knew It"; *Abraham Lincoln Assoc. Papers,* Springfield, Ill.: Abraham Lincoln Assoc., 1937. (Boston reports record of a trip in 1847.)

Pratt, Harry E.: " 'Judge' Abraham Lincoln"; *Journal of Ill. State Hist. Soc.,* XLVIII: 1, 28-39, Spring, 1955.

——: *Lincoln Day-by-Day 1809-1839* (Vol.1): Springfield, Ill.: Abraham Lincoln Assoc., 1941. (With Vols. 2-4, *Day-by-Day Activities* covers 1809-1861.) *See* also Angle, and Thomas.

——: *Lincoln Day-by-Day 1840-1846* (Vol. 2); Springfield, Ill.: Abraham Lincoln Assoc., 1939. (With Vols. 1, 3 and 4, *Day-by-Day Activities,* covers 1809-1861.) *See* also Angle, and Thomas.

——: *Lincolniana in the Illinois State Historical Library,* reprinted from Winter, 1953, Jr. of Ill. State Hist. Soc.; Springfield: State of Illinois, 1954.

——, ed.: *Lincoln's Inner Circle;* Springfield: Ill. State Hist. Library, 1955.

——: *Lincoln's Springfield;* Springfield: Ill. State Hist. Soc., 1955.

——: *The Personal Finances of Abraham Lincoln;* Springfield, Ill.: Abraham Lincoln Assoc., 1943. (Indispensable for this topic.)

Pratt, Marion Dolores: *See* Basler, Roy P.

Randall, James G.: *Constitutional Problems Under Lincoln* (revised ed.); New York: Appleton, 1926. (Basic and scholarly.)

——: "Lincoln and the Governance of Men"; *Abraham Lincoln Quarterly,* VI:6, 327-352, June, 1951. (Depicts Lincoln as human ruler.)

——: *Lincoln the Liberal Statesman;* New York: Dodd, Mead & Co., 1947. (Depicts human side of Lincoln's statesmanship.)

——: *Lincoln the President* (4 vols.); New York: Dodd, Mead & Co., 1945-1955. (Indispensable, critical but sympathetic; well documented.)

——: *Lincoln and the South;* Baton Rouge: Louisiana State Univ. Press, 1945.

——: "When the War Came in 1861"; *Abraham Lincoln Quarterly,* 1:1, 3-42, March, 1940. (The Fort Sumter decisions.)

Randall, Ruth Painter: *Mary Lincoln: Biography of a Marriage;* Boston: Little, Brown & Co., 1953. (Intimate in style, very helpful, documented.)

——: "Mary Lincoln: Judgment Appealed"; *Abraham Lincoln Quarterly,* V:7, 379-404, Sept., 1949.

——: *Lincoln's Sons;* Boston: Little, Brown & Co., 1955. (An excellent and reliable portrayal.)

Reep, Thomas P.: *Lincoln at New Salem;* Petersburg, Ill.: Old Salem Lincoln League, 1927. (New Salem as Lincoln knew it.)

Richmond, Mabel E.: *Centennial History of Decatur and Macon County;* Decatur: Herald-Review Publishers, 1931. (Excellent.)

Riddle, Albert Gallatin: *Recollections of War Times: Reminiscences of Men and Events in Washington 1860-1865;* New York: Putnam, 1895. (Lincoln's moves in behalf of the 13th Amendment.)

Robinson, Luther E.: *Abraham Lincoln as a Man of Letters;* Chicago: Reilly-Britton Co., 1918.

Russell, William Howard: *My Diary, North and South* (2 vols.); Boston: T.O.H.P. Burnham, 1863. (Considered a classic.)

Sandburg, Carl: *Abraham Lincoln: The Prairie Years* (2 vols.); New York: Harcourt, Brace & Co., 1926.

———: *Abraham Lincoln: The War Years* (4 vols.); New York: Harcourt, Brace & Co., 1939.

———: *Abraham Lincoln: The Prairie Years and the War Years* (1 vol. ed.); New York: Harcourt, Brace & Co., 1954.

———: *See* Meserve, Frederick Hill.

Sandburg, Carl, and Angle, Paul: *Mary Lincoln, Wife and Widow;* New York: Harcourt Brace, 1932-5.

Scripps, John Locke: *Life of Abraham Lincoln,* with forword and notes by M. L. Houser; Peoria, Ill.: Edward J. Jacob, 1931. (Based on autobiographical sketch furnished by Abraham Lincoln, and approved by him. Now included in Basler, et al., *Complete Works of Abraham Lincoln,* IV, 60-68.)

Shaw, Albert: *Abraham Lincoln: A Cartoon History* (2 vols.); New York: Review of Reviews Corp., 1929.

Shaw, Archer H., ed.: *The Lincoln Encyclopedia: The Spoken and Written Words of A. Lincoln,* Arranged for Ready Reference; New York: Macmillan Co., 1950. (Use with caution, contains some errors.)

Shannon, Fred A.: *The Organization and Administration of the Union Army, 1861-1865* (2 vols.); Cleveland: Arthur H. Clark Co., 1928.

Sharp, William: *Sonnets of This Century;* London: W. Scott, 1886. (Contains a most valuable history and technique of the sonnet.)

Shutes, Milton H.: *Lincoln and the Doctors, A Medical Narrative of the Life of Abraham Lincoln;* New York: Pioneer Press, 1933.

Smith, T. V.: *Abraham Lincoln and the Spiritual Life;* Boston: Beacon Press, 1951.

Sparks, Edwin Earle, ed.: *The Lincoln-Douglas Debates of 1858;* Springfield: Ill. State Hist. Library, 1908.

Stampp, Kenneth M.: *And the War Came: The North and the Secession Crisis 1860-1861;* Baton Rouge: Louisiana State Univ. Press, 1950. (No sectional harmony with slavery.)

Starr, John W., Jr.: *Lincoln and the Railroads: A Biographical Study;* New York: Dodd, Mead & Co., 1927.

——: *Lincoln's Last Day;* New York: Frederick A. Stokes Co., 1922. (*See* also Bryan, and Eisenschiml.)

Stern, Philip Van Doren: *The Life and Writings of Abraham Lincoln;* New York: Random House, 1940. *See* also Basler, et. al., *Collected Works.*

Stevenson, Augusta: *Abe Lincoln, Frontier Boy;* Indianapolis: Bobbs-Merrill, 1932. (Entertaining; portrays pioneer environment.)

Stoddard, William O.: *Inside the White House in War Times;* New York: Charles L. Webster & Co., 1890.

Sydnor, Charles S.: *The Development of Southern Sectionalism, 1819-1848;* Baton Rouge: Louisiana State Univ. Press, 1948. (Clarifies growth of this problem.)

Tarbell, Ida M.: *The Early Life of Abraham Lincoln;* New York: S. S. McClure, Limited, 1896. (Contains many unpublished documents and reminiscences of Lincoln's early friends.)

——: *In the Footsteps of the Lincolns;* New York: Harper & Brothers, 1924. (Indispensable; truthful, reliable and very helpful.)

——: *The Life of Abraham Lincoln* (4 vols.); New York: Lincoln History Society, 1902. (Truthful, inspirational and reliable account by one of the greatest of Lincoln authors.)

Teillard, Dorothy Lamon: *Recollections of Abraham Lincoln, 1847-1865, by Ward Hill Lamon;* Chicago: A. C. McClurg and Co., 1896. (Written by the daughter of Ward Hill Lamon from his notes. Lamon accompanied Lincoln to Washington and was appointed by Lincoln as Marshal of Washington during the War, 1860-1865.)

Thomas, Benjamin P.: *Abraham Lincoln: A Biography;* New York: Alfred A. Knopf, 1952. (Indispensable, reliable, succinct; based on Abraham Lincoln Association findings.)

——: "The Eighth Judicial Circuit"; *Abraham Lincoln Assoc. Bull.,* 40: 3-9, Sept., 1935.

——: "The Individuality of Lincoln as Revealed in His Writings"; *Abraham Lincoln Assoc. Bull.,* 32: 3-10, Sept., 1933.

——: *Lincoln, 1847-1853: Being the Day-by-Day Activities of Abraham Lincoln from January 1, 1947 to December 31, 1853* (Vol. 3); Springfield, Ill.: Abraham Lincoln Assoc., 1936. (With Vols. 1, 2 and 4, *Day-by-Day Activities* covers 1809-1861.) *See* also Angle, and Pratt.

——: "Lincoln's Earlier Practice in the Federal Courts 1839-1854"; *Abraham Lincoln Assoc. Bull.,* 39: 3-9, June, 1935.

——: *Lincoln's New Salem* (New and revised); New York: Alfred A. Knopf, 1954.

——: *Portrait for Posterity: Lincoln and His Biographers;* New Brunswick: Rutgers Univ. Press, 1947. (Indispensable; major Lincoln biographers discussed and evaluated: a guide to reliability of their work.)

———: "Lincoln: Voter and Candidate, 1831-1849"; *Abraham Lincoln Assoc. Bull.,* 36: 3-9, and 37: 3-9, Sept. and Dec., 1934.

Townsend, William H., "Lincoln's Defense of Duff Armstrong"; *American Bar Assoc. Journal,* 11: 81-84, 1925.

Townsend, George A.: "Lincoln's 'Rebel' Niece—Katherine Helm, Artist and Author"; *Lincoln Herald,* Feb., 1945.

Townsend, William T.: *Lincoln and His Wife's Home Town;* Indianapolis: Bobbs-Merrill, 1929. (Mary Lincoln's Southern ancestry and Lexington, Ky. background.)

———: *Lincoln and Liquor;* New York: Press of the Pioneers, 1934.

Turner, William E.: *On Abraham Lincoln's Trail from Hodgenville to Springfield;* Evansville, Ind.: Turner Publishing Co., 1930. (Excellent.)

Villard, Harold G. and Oswald Garrison, eds.: *Lincoln on the Eve of '61;* New York: Alfred A. Knopf, 1941. (A journalist's observation as he rode the Lincoln Special and reported the Lincoln speeches enroute to Washington, D. C. in 1861.)

Villard, Henry: *Memoirs of Henry Villard* (2 vols.); New York: Houghton, Mifflin & Co., 1904. (The above journalist.)

Weik, Jesse W.: *See* Herndon, William H.

Wakefield, Sherman D.: *How Lincoln Became President;* New York: Wilson-Erickson, 1936.

Walton, Clyde C.: *Illinois' Lincoln Letters;* Springfield: Ill. State Hist. Library, 1963.

Warren, Louis A.: *Lincoln's Parentage and Childhood;* New York: The Century Co., 1926. (A History of the Kentucky Lincolns supported by documentary evidence; helps to redeem Tom Lincoln. Indispensable.)

———: "Hananiah Lincoln in Revolution and Pioneer History"; *Indiana Magazine of History,* March, 1929. Bloomington, Ind.: Indiana Univ. Press. (Helpful.)

——: "The Environs of Lincoln's Youth"; Springfield, Ill.: *Abraham Lincoln Assoc. Papers,* pp. 111-144, Feb. 12, 1932.

——: *Lincoln's Youth, Indiana Years: 1816-1830;* Indianapolis: Indiana Hist. Soc., 1959. (Covers seven to twenty-one, 1816-1830.)

——: "The Romance of Thomas Lincoln and Nancy Hanks"; *Indiana Magazine of History,* XXX: 3, 213-222, Sept., 1934. (Helpful.)

Weaver, George Sumner: *Lives and Graves of our Presidents;* Chicago: Elder Pub. Co., 1884. (Chiefly biographical sketches.)

Whitney, Henry C.: *Life on the Circuit with Lincoln;* Caldwell, Idaho: Claxton Printers, 1892. (His observations colorfully presented.)

Williams, Kenneth P.: *Lincoln Finds a General: A Military Study of the Civil War;* New York: Macmillan Co., 1949-1952. (Excellent; Lincoln's strategy and his generals.)

Williams, T. Harry: *Lincoln and His Generals;* New York: Alfred A. Knopf, 1952. (Convincing recognition of Lincoln as a strategist.)

——: *Lincoln and the Radicals;* Madison: Univ. of Wisconsin Press, 1941.

Wilson, Rufus Rockwell: *Lincoln in Caricature;* Elmira, N. Y.: Primavera Press, 1945.

Woldman, Albert A.: *Lawyer Lincoln;* Boston: Houghton Mifflin, 1936.

Wood, Clement: *Poet's Handbook;* Garden City: Garden City Pub. Co., 1942. (Excellent; indispensable for understanding of the sonnet.)

Wood, Clement: *Wood's Unabridged Rhyming Dictionary;* Cleveland, Ohio: World Pub. Co., 1943.

Zane, John M.: "Lincoln the Constitutional Lawyer"; *Abraham Lincoln Assoc. Papers,* pp. 27-108, Feb. 12, 1932.

PERIODICALS

Abraham Lincoln Association Bulletin (published quarterly); Springfield, Ill.: Abraham Lincoln Assoc., 1924-1939.

Abraham Lincoln Association Papers; Springfield, Ill.: Abraham Lincoln Assoc., 1924-1939. (Delivered before the members of the Lincoln Assoc.)

Abraham Lincoln Quarterly; Springfield, Ill.: Abraham Lincoln Assoc., 1940—

American Bar Association Journal; Chicago, Ill.: American Bar Association.

American Magazine (monthly); New York: Crowell-Collier.

American Historical Review (quarterly); New York: Macmillan Co.

Century Magazine; New York: Scribner & Co. 1870-81; New York: Century Co. 1881-1930.

Harper's Weekly (a journal of civilization); Vol. 1-62, Jan. 3, 1857-Apr. 29, 1916. New York: Harper & Brothers.

Illinois History (A magazine published monthly during school year, October through May); Springfield: Illinois State Historical Library.

Indiana Magazine of History (published quarterly); Bloomington: Dept. of History of Indiana University in cooperation with Indiana Historical Society.

Journal of the Illinois State Historical Society; Springfield: Illinois State Historical Society.

Lincoln Centennial Association Papers; Springfield, Ill.: Lincoln Centennial Assoc., 1924-1928.

Lincoln Herald (quarterly); Harrogate, Tenn.: Lincoln Memorial Univ. Press.

The Lincoln Kinsman (published monthly); Fort Wayne, Ind. (Box 1110): Lincolniana Publishers, 1938—

Lincoln Lore (published weekly); Fort Wayne, Ind.: Lincoln National Life Insurance Co., 1929—

Leslie's Illustrated Weekly Newspaper; Vols. 1-91, 93-94, Dec. 15, 1855-Dec. 22, 1900; July 6, 1901-June 26, 1902. New York: Frank Leslie, editor and publisher.

St. Nicholas Magazine; New York: Scribner Co., 1873-1881; New York: Century Co., 1881-1940. (A monthly magazine for boys and girls.)

Papers in Illinois History; Springfield, Ill.: Illinois State Hist. Soc.

Saturday Evening Post (weekly); Philadelphia, Pa.: Curtis Pub. Co.

Transactions of Illinois State Historical Society; Springfield, Ill.: Ill. State Hist. Soc.

INDEX

This volume's cross-index affords a narrative guide to *both* the Lincoln story *and* Lincoln-Hanks genealogy and migrations.

Abraham: *Lincoln* line, progenitor Samuel's grandson, by son Mordecai Sr., first to bear name of, 20, 22-25; Mordecai Sr.'s grandson, by son Mordecai Jr., bore name of, as husband of Daniel Boone's cousin, Anne Boone, 25, 29, 157; Mordecai Jr.'s grandson, by son "Virginia John," bore name of, as a captain of frontier militia, 36-40; Captain Abraham's to-be-President grandson, by son Thomas (and Nancy Hanks), bore name of, 36, 70; features of, found, 33; Nancy told her "Abe" the Bible story of, 75; name of, also in *Hanks* line, many generations, 70, 166-167.

Adams, Samuel: "Boston Tea Party," a Lincoln also there, 28, 31.

Amity, Pa.: Mary Robeson of, 2nd wife of Mordecai Jr., 25.

Ancestors: Lincoln-Hanks, line of, 5; homes of, photos, 14c; maps locating, 16, 24, 36; *see* Genealogy, Migration.

Anderson Creek: *see* Creek.

Animals: sounds, habits of, 77-78; prowling of, 88; rout of, 89; deer, 63, 128; Abe's dog, 132; in deep snow, 148.

Bacon's Rebellion: 1676, Thomas Hanks missing thereafter, 50.

Barlow, Catherine: Abe's uncle Josiah Lincoln's wife, 40, 85.

Beechland: Washington Co., Ky., Hanks', Berrys' home, 58, 59.

Berkeley, Sir William: Governor of Virginia Colony, precipitated Bacon's Rebellion—refused aid against Indians, 50.

Berry, Richard: Hanks' neighbor, husband of Polly Ewing who employed Nancy Hanks, 58; Tom Lincoln and Nancy Hanks wed in home of, bond signed by, as Nancy's guardian, 59.

Birds: doves, 63; thrush, 69; song of, 74, 78, 79, 107; geese, 87; turkey, pigeons, 90; sounds of, 109, 130.

Block House: wilderness inn, fortified against Indians, 36.

Books: Nancy told stories from, 75; Nancy read from, 92; Abe memorized from, 96; teacher urged improved reading of, 97; six, in Lincoln library, 100; Sarah interceded for Abe's love of, 113; arithmetic, spelling, 115; *Indiana Statutes,* 118; history, 120; Abe read Bible, 144; Illinois laws, 150.

Boone, Anne: wife of Abraham Lincoln, Mordecai Jr.'s and Mary's son, 29.

Boone, Daniel: own cousin of Anne and William Boone, 29.

Boone, George: neighbor of Mordecai Lincoln Jr., 29.

Boone, Sarah (Lincoln): wife of Wm. Boone, George's son, 29.

Boone, Squire: Lincolns, neighbors of; pride, hospitality of; Daniel, George, sons of; Dan cut Wilderness Rd. to Ky., 29, 36.

Boone, William: wed Sarah Lincoln, Mordecai Jr.'s daughter, 29.

"Boston Tea Party": Amos Lincoln, Samuel Adams took part, 28.

Bound Brook: boundary line between Hingham and Scituate, Mass.; Cohasset side, site of Mordecai Lincoln Sr.'s Iron Works, 22; Scituate side, promontory, site of Mordecai Sr.'s home, 16, 23.

Braintree, Mass.: Mary Chapin of, Mordecai Sr.'s 2nd wife, 16, 23.

British: in Boston Bay, ships of, unjust tax of, 27-28; taxes on colonial industry, 31; decrees of, rebellion against, 32.

Brumfield, William: husband of Nancy Lincoln, Abe's aunt, 85.

Buckhorn Manor: Middletown, N. J., Mordecai Jr.'s forge at, 24.

Burial: of Captain Abraham Lincoln, 95; of Abe's mother, 105.

Bush, Sarah: Sarah Johnston Lincoln, Abe's stepmother, 111.

Cabin: photos of, 14c-h; Captain Abraham Lincoln's, 40; Tom's and Nancy's in Elizabethtown, Ky., 60; furnished by Tom, 61; Nolin Creek, Abe's birthplace, 63-64; Knob Creek, scene of Abe's childhood, 74; lack of, 88; on hillside crest, 90; Pigeon Creek, site of Abe's youth, 99; on Sangamon, 138.

Index 203

Cabinet-making: Tom Lincoln's, 57, 72, 125, 139; cash for, 63, 72.

Camp: enroute to Indiana, 86; half-face, 1816-1817 home, 88; enroute to Illinois, 131.

Chapin, Mary: 2nd wife of Mordecai Lincoln, Sr., 23.

Charles the First: King of England, 18; life under rule of, Thomas Lincoln's opinion of, 19; tyrant, befools Parliament, 20; Thomas Hanks' opposition of, with Cromwell; death of, 49.

Charleston, Ill.: in Coles Co.; Dennis Hanks, Levi Hall families' home, 151; Tom Lincoln's last home, 14h, 68, 151-152.

Church: photos of, 14b; Lincolns', in Hingham, Norfolk, England, 14b; "Old Ship," progenitor Samuel Lincoln's, in Hingham, Mass., 14b, 21; Tom Lincoln took Nancy Hanks to, 58; "Little Mound" Baptist, on Knob Creek, 14b, 76, 79, 83, 106; lack of, 91; need of, 92, 126; Lincoln names on books of, 98; "Little Pigeon," on Pigeon Creek, Spencer Co., Ind., 14b, 98.

Coffin-maker: Tom Lincoln as, 60, with Abe, for Nancy, 105; Tom teaches Abe and Dennis Hanks, trade of, 124-126.

Cohasset, Mass.: home of Mordecai Sr. and Martha, 22, 23, 156.

County: *In Ky.,* Hardin, 46, 57, 68; Jefferson, 14c, 37-38; Lincoln, 38-39; Nelson, 53, 162; Washington, 42, 46, 57, 59, 161. *In Ill.,* Coles, 14h, 137, 151; Macon, 14g. *In Ind.,* Spencer, 14e, 68, 82. *In Pa.,* Berks, 14c, 26, 29, 33, 35. *In Va.,* Gloucester, 51; Hampton (now Mineral, W. Va.), 53, 162; Richmond, 51-53; Rockingham, 30, 36.

Court House: in Springfield, Ky., Nancy Hanks' marriage bond, treasure of, 59; in Rockport, Ind., Tom Lincoln's entry in Tract Book, 82; in Relic Room, cabinet made by Tom, 125, 173.

Crawford, Andrew: Abe's first teacher at Pigeon Creek, 97, 120.

Crawford, Elizabeth: cabinet-maker Tom Lincoln and, 125.

Creek: *Anderson,* in Spencer Co., Ind., Abe ran Taylor's ferry at mouth of, 68, 121, 173; *Floyd's,* in Jefferson Co., Ky., site of Hughes' Station, 14c, 36-38; *Knob,* near Hodgenville, Ky., and Little Mound Church, 14b; Abe's childhood home, 14d, 68, 74-76, 79, 81, 106, 167; *Linville,* in Shenandoah Valley, Va., Rockingham Co., site of homes of "Virginia John" and his son Jacob Lincoln, 14c, 24, 30, 36; *Mill,* in Hardin Co., Ky., site of first farm owned by Tom Lincoln, 46, 68; *Nolin,* site of Abe's birthplace cabin near Hodgenville, Ky., 14d, 63, 68; *Patterson's,* in Hampton Co., Va. (now Mineral Co., W. Va.), site of birthplace of Abe's mother, on Mike's Run of, 24, 36, 53 (162); *Pigeon,* in Spencer Co., Ind., site of Little Pigeon Church, 14b, and home of Abe's youth, 14e-f, 68; Tom's decision to move to, 81; claim staked in primal territory of, 82; site of half-face camp where Abe learned use of axe, 89; school life at, 97; *Pottinger's,* site of Nelson Co., Ky., farm of Joseph Hanks, on Rolling Fork of Salt River near mouth of, 53, 162, 167.

Cromwell's Civil War: Tom Hanks fought King Charles I in, 49.

Crowder, Sterling: Hananiah Lincoln and, fought together in 1777, at battle of Brandywine, 44, 160.

Crume, Mary (Lincoln): Abe's aunt, Ralph Crume's wife, 85.

Crume, Ralph: married Mary Lincoln, Tom's sister, 85

Cumberland Gap: Capt. Lincoln passed through, on Wilderness Road, 36.

Decatur, Macon Co., Ill.: 1830, the Lincolns' arrival at, 134.

Deep Snow, Winter of the: December 1830-March 1831, suffering, food lack, floods of, 148-151.

Dorsey, Azel W.: Abe's 2nd teacher at Pigeon Creek, Ind., 115.

Downs, Rev. Wm.: 1816, immersed Tom Lincoln in Knob Creek, 76.

Elizabethtown: ('Lisbuthtown, E-town), in Hardin Co., Ky.; Tom Lincoln takes bride Nancy Hanks to, 59; Tom makes home at, 60; maps showing, 68; farewell visit to, by Tom and Nancy, 84.

Index

Elkins, Parson David: prays at farewell dinner for Lincolns, 83; is "St. John of the Wilderness," letter to and from, conducts memorial service for Abe's mother, 106.

England: Hingham, 16, 18; Malmesbury, 16, 49; Britain of, brothers, skilled craftsmen, Thomas and Daniel Lincoln leave, for New England; brother Samuel follows, 18, 19; unjust colonial taxes of, 27; view of colonists, 31; with France, war of, 45; flag of, 122.

Enlow, Abraham: sent for granny woman when Abe was born, 69.

Exeter: Berks Co., Pa., home of Lincolns and Boones, 26, 29, 157.

Flowers, Rebecca: Mrs. Morris, whom "Virginia John" wed, 30.

Floyd's Creek: *see* Creek.

Food, nature of: at "infare" of Tom and Nancy, 59; on claim-staking trip to Ind., 82; from garden and forest, 88; of pioneers, 90; lack of, in Winter of the Deep Snow, 149.

Fowke, Capt. Thomas: brought Thomas Hanks to Va., 49.

France: aid in Revolutionary War, recognized by, 45; flag of, 122.

Freedom: rights of, 18; of religion, 23; where reigns, 24; Hananiah Lincoln's view of, 45; from slavery; equal rights of, 81; ills of lack of, 116; guarantees of, 118.

Friend, Charles: father of Dennis Friend Hanks, 70, 166.

Genealogy: Lincoln-Hanks, generations of, 5; blood saviours of America, search and proof of, 17; Abe Lincoln, President in '61, six generations from progenitor Samuel Lincoln, 21; of first *Abraham* Lincoln, 22; Lincoln traits, features, survival of, 33; of President Abraham Lincoln, 34.

Gentry, James: Abe and, flatboat trip to New Orleans, 122.

Gentryville: Spencer Co., Ind., Abe's home (1816-1830) close to, when at Pigeon Creek, 68, 88-128.

Gollaher, Austin: Abe's playmate at Knob Creek, 77-78.

Graham, Dr. Christopher Columbus: at Abe-Nancy "infare," 59, 164.

Green River: site of Capt. Abraham's Lincoln Co. land, 38, 158.

Grigsby, Aaron: "neglect" of wife Sarah, Abe's sister, 123.

Grigsby, Sarah (Lincoln): birth of, 61; baby clothes of, 66; goes to school with brother Abe, learns from mother, 75; loneliness of, 107; struggles, to wash and cook, mother's care needs of, 108; death of, 123. *See* Lincoln, Sarah.

Hall, Levi: wed Nancy Hanks, aunt of Abe's mother, 70, 166.

Hall, Nancy (Hanks): mother of Dennis Friend Hanks, 70, 166.

Hall, Squire: son of Levi; wed Matilda Johnston, Abe's stepsister, 111.

Hanks, Ann (Lee): wed Joseph Hanks Sr., Abe's mother was granddaughter of, 52; widowhood, visit to son Tom in Va., death of, 55.

Hanks, Catherine (—): wife of John (1690?-1740), mother of Joseph Sr. (1725-1793), 5, 52.

Hanks, Dennis Friend: photo of, 14g; cousin of Abe's mother, reared with her in home of Tom and Betty (Hanks) Sparrow; at birth of Nancy Hanks Lincoln's first boy, joy of; asks baby's name, 70; Tom Lincoln's home, care of, 109; pledge of Abe's mother, at death of foster parents of, 110; wed Elizabeth Johnston, Abe's stepsister, 111; taught by Tom Lincoln, 125; lost stock by milk sickness, 126; moved to Coles Co., Ill., 137.

Hanks, Elizabeth (Johnston): wife of Dennis Friend Hanks, 111.

Hanks, Elizabeth: daughter of Joseph and Ann. *See* Sparrow, Elizabeth (Hanks).

Hanks, John: (1690?-1740), son of William (1650?-1704); wed Catherine, built large estate; Joseph Sr. (1725-1793) son of, 5, 52.

Hanks, John: photo of, 14g; first cousin of Abe's mother, as grandson of Joseph and Ann by their son William; report of, about Illinois, 127; home of, near Decatur, Ill., 134; Lincolns, welcome of, 135; planning of, for Lincoln cabin, 137; Abe splits rails with, 145; trip agreement of, 152, 175,

Index

Hanks, Joseph Sr.: (1725-1793), son of John (1690?-1740), 5; wed Ann Lee; daughter Lucy crushed pride of; moved from Richmond Co. to Hampton Co., Va., then to Nelson Co., Ky., with Lucy and her child: gossip follows, 52-54; death of, 55.

Hanks, Joseph Jr.: son of Joseph Sr. (1725-1793), brother of Lucy (1766-1825), 5; uncle of Abe's mother, wed Polly Young; assigns inherited land to brother William, begins woodcraft career, 55; shows Tom Lincoln cabinet-making methods, 57; takes Tom in as apprentice, 60; entertains Tom and Nancy, 84.

Hanks, Lucy: (1766-1825), daughter of Joseph Sr. (1725-1793), 5, 54; in Richmond Co., Va., crushed her father's pride, and in Hampton Co., Va. (now Mineral Co., W. Va.) gave birth to Abe's mother, Nancy Hanks (1783-1818), 162; aroused gossip, went with her father and child to Nelson Co., Ky., bore pity, gossip, 53-54; wed Henry Sparrow, 55; earned praise, 162.

Hanks, Nancy: Lucy's sister, thus aunt of Abe's mother; wife of Levi Hall; mother of Dennis Friend Hanks and Squire Hall, 52, 55, 70.

Hanks, Nancy: (1783-1818), granddaughter of Joseph and Ann by their daughter Lucy (1766-1825), 5, 162; wife of Thomas Lincoln (1778-1851), 5, 53-56; mother of Abraham Lincoln (1809-1865), 5, 69-70. *See* Lincoln, Nancy (Hanks).

Hanks, Sarah (Woodbridge): wife of William Sr. (1650?-1704), mother of William Jr., Luke, *and* John (1690?-1740), 5, 51.

Hanks, Thomas: (1630?-1676?) of Malmesbury, England, and of Gloucester Co., Va.; fought in Cromwell's Civil War against King Charles I; sent into servitude, sold to colonist, 5, 49; free, large proprietor, 1653; probable victim of Bacon's Rebellion or Indian raids, 1676, no further trace of, 50; credited progenitor of Hanks line, 5, 51.

Hanks, Thomas: eldest son of Joseph and Ann; from Richmond

Co., went ahead of family to Hampton Co., Va. (now Mineral Co., W. Va.), joined there by his parents and their eight other children, 36, 55, 162; when Joseph Sr. died, Ann returned to, 55.

Hanks, William: (1650?-1704), carpenter in Richmond Co., Va., probably of Thomas Hanks' (1630?-1676?) family who lived across the Rappahannock River in Gloucester Co., Va.; Sarah Woodbridge, wife of; William, Luke, John, sons of; large estate of, 5, 51.

Hazel, Caleb: Abe's 2nd teacher at Knob Creek, 75.

Head, Rev. Jesse: read marriage vows when Thomas Lincoln wed Nancy Hanks, wrote nuptial bond and marriage return, 59.

Herring, Bathsheba: wife of Capt. Abraham Lincoln (1744-1786), 5, 35. *See* Lincoln, Bathsheba (Herring).

Hickory Point: John Hanks' home near Decatur, Ill., 135, 137.

Hingham, Mass.: first American home of Lincolns, 16, 18, 155.

Hingham, Norfolk Co., England: Lincolns came from, 16, 18, 155.

Hodgenville, Ky.: Tom Lincoln's land and cabin, Abe's birthplace, near, 63; Christmas Eve in cabin near, 64; Tom walks to, about lien, 72; map showing, 68; farewell visit to, 84.

Hughes' Station: Floyd's Creek, Jefferson Co., Ky., location of; in 1786, home of Capt. Abraham Lincoln, 14c, 36, 38.

Hull, Mass.: Mordecai Lincoln's bride, Sarah Jones, from, 16, 22.

Illinois: photos of, 14a,g,h; map of, and route to, 68; John Hanks writes Tom Lincoln about small poverty, good soil, no milk sickness of, Tom's decision to move to, setting out for, 127-128; soil, birds, flowers of, 130-131; spring rains, mud of, 133; home, life of Lincolns in Macon Co. of, 134-153; rolling land of, 134; Abe envisions rich crops of, 140; Tom plans to move from Macon to Coles Co. of, 151. *See* Lincoln, Abraham (Abe), Thomas (Tom).

Index

Indiana: photos of, 14e,d; map of, and route to, and from, 68; better land titles, slavery outlawed in, 81, 118; home, life of Lincolns in Spencer Co., of, 88-128; wilds, hard life, loneliness, food of, 88-91, 107-110, 114; schools and churches of, 92-98, 106, 115-117; deadly illness of, 103-104, 124-126. *See* Lincoln, Abraham (Abe), Thomas (Tom).

Indians: colonists and a Lincoln disguise as, 28; intent on war, 36; maps including haunts of Indians, 24, 36; Virginia pledged protection from; contract fee misunderstood by, their giving possession of Kentucky lands as contracted refused by, 37; scorn of, for Captain Lincoln, want his scalp to save their lands, 38; malice of, against life of Capt. Abraham, 40; Tom Lincoln rescued from, 41; raids of, and Bacon's Rebellion, 50; cruelty, misunderstanding, killing of father by, related by Tom Lincoln as he tells children of, 94-95; killings by, ceasing, 80; friendship of, 132; Abe's memory of, 136.

Johnston, Elizabeth: Abe's stepsister; wed Dennis Hanks, 111.

Johnston, John D.: Abe's stepbrother, 111-112, 127, 137, 152.

Johnston, Matilda: Abe's stepsister; wed Squire Hall, 111.

Johnston, Sarah (Bush): in 1819, wed Thomas Lincoln, 111.

Jones, *Abraham:* first *Abraham* Lincoln named for, 22.

Jones, Sarah: of Hull, Mass., daughter of *Abraham,* first wife of Mordecai Lincoln Sr., mother of Mordecai Jr. and *Abraham,* 22; death of, 23.

Jones, Will: storekeeper in Gentryville, Abe worked for, 120.

Kentucky: photos of, 14b,c,d; maps of 36, 68; Hanks' homes in, 53-86; Lincoln homes in, 37-46, 57-86; good soil of, 38-39; hardships of, 37-42; poor land titles of, 72, 81; detriments of and opposition to slavery in, 76, 80. *See* County; Hanks; Lincoln; Migration.

Knob Creek: photos of, 14b,d; map showing, 68; location of, Tom Lincoln's farm and cabin on Louisville turnpike at, 74; first school attended by Abe and Sarah Lincoln, 75; Rev. Wm.

Downs immersed Tom Lincoln in, 76; Lincoln neighbors at, 77; life of, Tommy Lincoln of, 79; Tom's decision to leave, 81.
Lee, Ann: Joseph Hanks Sr.'s wife, of Robert Lee line, 52, 55.
Lincoln, Abraham: *see* Lincoln, Mordecai Sr., and Sarah (Jones).
Lincoln, Abraham: *see* Lincoln, Mordecai Jr., Mary (Robeson).
Lincoln, Abraham (Captain): (1744-1786), 5; eldest son of "Virginia John" and Rebecca, militia guard of Shenandoah homesteads from Indians, wed Bathsheba Herring, 30, 33, 35; Old Virginia's honor of; taking Bathsheba and son Thomas (1778-1851), 5, travels Wilderness Road to Ky., 36; quiets Indian uprisings, 39; near fort, land, cabin of, 14c, 37; Indian hatred of, 38; while corn planting, death of, by Indians, 40; Tom's rescue by Mordecai and Josiah, older sons of, 41; Tom tells his children of, 94-95.
Lincoln, Abraham (Abe): (1809-1865), vii, 5; pioneer boy, 3; photos, maps, pertaining to, 14a-h, 16, 24, 36, 68; of six generations from progenitor Samuel Lincoln, President in '61, short schooled, eager to learn, like Sam, 21; birth of, 69, 70; boyhood impressions of, 71; first school, teachers, teaching of; Mother Nancy's home teaching of, 75; Knob hills church attendance, religious impressions, rebellion of, 76; Austin Gollaher, playmate of, 77; with Austin, learns about woods creatures and crafts from Tom, father of, 78; learns cause and regret of Tom's lost father's love, 89; food of, 90; home schooling of, 93; memorizing, character development of, 96; at Pigeon Creek, Andrew Crawford's teaching of, 97; feels prejudice of preachers' creedal fury, 98; has place in new cabin loft, 99; reads Lincoln library, 100; grief of, at mother's death and burial, 104-105; helps make mother's coffin, 105; writes letter to minister, 106; grief, loneliness of, 107; at Tom's long absence, wonder and fear of, 109; stepmother notes intellectual eagerness of, 113; Lincoln creed learned by, 114; at school when fourteen, thirst for knowledge, champion spelling of, 115; clerk-

ing in Will Jones' store, reading papers, writing against slavery, liquor, and verse-writing of, 116; early speeches of, 117; reads *Indiana Statutes,* desires to serve, 118; stature of, 119; help, work, character, reading of, 120; ferryboat work, wages, other compensations of, 121; takes produce on flatboat to New Orleans, impressions of, 122; at sister Sarah's death, emotions of, 123; from New Orleans, return of; helps Tom make coffins, 124-125; at mother's grave, 128; enroute to Illinois, 128-134; height, features of, 135; recalls past, has vision of his future— with cross at end, 136; helps stepmother make flower bed, 138; breaks sod, plants seed, 140; girl friends of, 142; dancing, story telling of, 143; self-analysis, Bible reading of, 144; rail splitting, fame of, 145; first (1830) political speech of, 146; accident of, guest at Sheriff Warnick's home; *Illinois Statutes,* reading of, 150; freed by Tom, to accept Offutt's offer, 152-153.

Lincoln, Amos: great-great-grandson of progenitor Samuel; took part in "Boston Tea Party," son found tea in shoes of, 28.

Lincoln, Anne (Boone): see Boone, Anne; Lincoln, Mary (Robeson).

Lincoln, Bathsheba (Herring): wed Capt. Abraham, is disinherited but happy, 35; journeys with husband via Wilderness Road to Ky., Tom on her lap, 36; widowed, moves to Washington Co., Ky., 40-42; is helped by Hananiah Lincoln, hears of war, 43-45; courage, teaching of, to her children, 46.

Lincoln, Catherine (Barlow): wed Josiah, Abe's uncle, 85.

Lincoln, Daniel: brother of Thomas and progenitor Samuel (1619-1690), 5, came with Tom to America, 19; bachelor, prodigal, willed all to brother Sam, 22.

Lincoln, Enoch: Governor of Maine, 34.

Lincoln, Hananiah: cousin of Capt. Lincoln; is rich, honest, sympathetic; helps widowed Bathsheba Lincoln and her children, 43; visits Bathsheba, tells of war, its causes, his fighting, 44-45.

Lincoln-Hanks: generations of, six ascending; descending, Lincolns only, 5; saviors of America, sources of, 17.

Lincoln, Hannah (Saltar): of Buckhorn Manor near Middletown, N. J.; gay, pretty heiress, first wife of Mordecai Jr., 24; death of, 25.

Lincoln, Jacob: son of "Virginia John" and Rebecca; remained on Linville Creek family land in Shenandoah Valley, Va., 14c, 24.

Lincoln, "Virginia John": (1716-1788), 5; eldest son of Mordecai Jr.; sells father's gift-land, moves to Shenandoah's vale; widow Rebecca (Flowers) Morris, wife of, 30; death, children, bequests of, 33.

Lincoln, Josiah: brother of Abe's father, wed Catherine Barlow, 40, 85.

Lincoln, Levi: Governor of Massachusetts, 34.

Lincoln, Levi Jr., also Governor of Massachusetts, 34.

Lincoln, Mary: sister of Abe's father, wed Ralph Crume, 85.

Lincoln, Mary (Chapin): 2nd wife of Mordecai Sr., 23.

Lincoln, Mary (Mudd): wife of Abe's uncle Mordecai, 85.

Lincoln, Mary (Robeson): 2nd wife of Mordecai Jr., cares for first wife Hannah's five children, and own three sons, 25; Abraham, son of, wed Anne Boone, 29.

Lincoln, Mordecai Sr.: (1657-1727), 5; son of progenitor Samuel and Martha; skilled as blacksmith, ironmonger; wed Sarah Jones, daughter of Abraham, of Hull, Mass.; Mordecai Jr., first child of; *Abraham* (first in Lincoln line), next child of, 22; Mary Chapin, of Braintree, Mass., 2nd wife of, 23.

Lincoln, Mordecai Jr.: (1686-1736), 5; son of Mordecai Sr. and Sarah; leaves home, taking brother Abraham, 23; builds forge on Buckhorn Manor near Middletown, N. J., weds owner's daughter, Hannah Saltar, 24; after Hannah's death, sees five children need care; weds Mary Robeson of Amity, Pa., who bears three sons of, 25; moves to Pa., builds showplace house; dies, at age of forty-nine, 26.

Lincoln, Mordecai: eldest son of Capt. Abraham and Bathsheba; kills father's slayer, rescues brother Thomas (1778-1851), 5, 41; heir-at-law of father's estate, 46; invites Tom and Nancy to visit, 84; Mary Mudd, wife of; makes home for Bathsheba, mother of; entertains Tom and Nancy, 85.

Lincoln (name): first of, in America, 19; Revolutionary soldiers, 335 of, 32; survives in Virginia, 33; on church books, 98; *Abraham,* brother of Mordecai Jr. (1686-1736), 5, 25; *Abraham,* Captain (1744-1786), 5, 35-40, 94-95; *Abraham* (Abe), President (1809-1865), vii, 3, 5, 21, 70, 71, 75-78, 93, 96-100, 104-106, 108-110, 112-125, 127-133, 135-138, 140-147, 150, 152-153.

Lincoln, Nancy: sister of Abe's father; Wm. Brumfield's wife, 85.

Lincoln, Nancy (Hanks): (1783-1818), daughter of Lucy Hanks (1766-1825), 5, 162; is taken with mother to Kentucky by Joseph Sr., grandfather of, 54; lives in home of Thomas and Elizabeth (Hanks) Sparrow, her aunt; sews, spins, reads, 56; Tom Lincoln's courting of, 58; wedding of, treasured marriage bond of, 59; has first child, 61; Nolin Creek cabin, happiness of, 63; wishes for son, 65; February 11, 1809, sewing of, 66; February 12, 1809, bears son, 69; names son *Abraham,* after grandfather, 70; meets Tom returning from Hodgenville, 73; held in Tom's arms, as they consider thrills of new Knob Creek home, 74; teaches children stories, games, Bible lore, 75; impresses her gospel of love on Abe, 76; bears 2nd son, Tommy; loses him, 79; "E-town," Hodgenville, farewell visits, 84, 85; travels to Indiana, 86-88; further teachings of, 92-93; cares for foster parents through milk sickness and death, 102-103; illness, death, burial of, 104-105, 126; memorial of, 106; Abe at grave of, 128; recalls mother's grave, 136.

Lincoln, Rebecca (Flowers): "Virginia John's" paragon wife, 30.

Lincoln, Samuel: (1619-1690), 5; born in Hingham, England; died in Hingham, Mass.; brother of Daniel and Thomas; is well trained weaver; *progenitor* of him who would redeem nation from slavery, 20; of sixth generation before Abe, President, 21; inherits Dan's property, buys more land, builds house, weds Martha; Mordecai Sr., son of, 22.

Lincoln, Sarah (Jones): first wife of Mordecai Sr., 22.

Lincoln, Sarah: Abe's sister; birth of, 61; attends school with Abe, 75; rides horse with mother, to Indiana, 86; hears parents tell stories, 93-95; bathes, dresses, and combs hair of mother's corpse, 105; lonely, stands by mother's grave, 107; too young to properly cook, wash, care for cabin, needs mother's care and help, 108; lonesome, 110; wife of Aaron Grigsby, "neglected" by him in childbirth, dies, 123. *See* Grigsby, Sarah (Lincoln).

Lincoln, Sarah (Bush) Johnston: 2nd wife of Thomas; stepmother of Abe and Sarah; widow with three children; arrives with Tom, moves into cabin; is kind, foresighted, good housekeeper, 111; glad welcome of, 112; shows interest in Abe's education, 113; flowers of, 138.

Lincoln, Thomas: *first Lincoln in America* (1633); craftsman; escapes English tyranny, brings brothers Dan and Sam, 18.

Lincoln, Thomas: (1778-1851), 5; born on Linville Creek, Rockingham Co., Va; died in Coles Co., Ill.; photos of homes of, 14c-h, churches of, 14b; *see* maps, 24, 36, 68, Migrations; son of Captain Abraham and Bathsheba; sits on mother's lap on Wilderness Road trip to Ky., 36; sees father killed by Indian, 40; is saved by brother's shot, 41; goes with widowed mother, Bathsheba, to Washington Co., Ky., 42; works out until twenty-eight; at twenty-five, buys 238 acres of land on Mill Creek, 46; sees need of a skill, asks Joseph Hanks Jr. to teach him woodcraft, as his apprentice, 57; woos, plans to wed Nancy Hanks; besides Mill Creek farm, owns lot and cabin in Elizabethtown, Ky., 58; weds Nancy, takes her to home in "E-town," 59-60; works out apprenticeship, makes coffins, 60; has first child, Sarah; wishes next for boy, 61; buys land with cabin on

Index 215

Nolin Creek, near Hodgenville, Ky., 63; with wife and child, Christmas Eve, 64; makes cradle, hopes for son, 65; sends neighbor for granny woman; February 12, 1809, has son, 69; worries about lien on farm, 72; fails to get privilege to substitute produce for cash, 73; finds farm on Knob Creek, bargains for it, moves, has four happy years, 74; teaches his son Abe and Austin Gollaher about woods creatures, 77-78; has son Tommy, and loses him to angel, 79; finds Ky. land titles bad, decides to move across the Ohio, 81; stakes claim near Pigeon Creek, in Spencer Co., Ind.; builds raft, plans move, 82; neighbors' farewell of, 83; with family and goods, makes farewell visit to "E-town" and Hodgenville relatives and friends, 84-85; moves family to Indiana, 86-87; builds half-face camp, 88; teaches Abe use of axe, 89; teaches his children history of Captain Lincoln's death and burial, 93-95; finishes cabin, 99, 101; at Nancy's death, builds her coffin, grieves, 105; is lonely, sees needs of home and children, 107-108; leaves home with Dennis Hanks in charge, 109; returns with new wife and her three children, 111; clears land, makes coffins, 114, 124-126; teaches Abe and Dennis coffin-making, 125; moves family to Illinois, 127-134; arrives at Sangamon, Decatur, Stevens' Creek, John Hanks' cabin, 134; welcome of, 135, 137; builds Sangamon cabin, 138; makes furniture, moves into cabin, 139; receives welcome of neighbors, 141; experiences Winter of Deep Snow hardships, 148-149, 151-152; decides to move to Coles Co., Ill., and let Abe go free, 151-152; bids Abe goodbye, 153.

Lincoln, Tommy: 2nd son of Tom and Nancy, dies in infancy, 79.

Linville Creek: *See* Creek.

Maine: Enoch Lincoln, governor of, 34.

Malaria: prevalent in Illinois, Lincolns suffer from, 149.

Malmesbury, England: progenitor Thomas Hanks from, 5, 16, 49.

Massachusetts: photos of, 14b-c; map of, 16; Lincolns in, Thomas (first Lincoln in America), Daniel, Samuel (progenitor), Mordecai Sr., Mordecai Jr., Abraham (first of that name), 18-23; Levi Sr. and Levi Jr., governors of; and others, 34.

Middletown, N. J.: Buckhorn Manor close to, 24.

Migration: maps, 16, 24, 36, 68; *Hanks—Thomas,* from Malmesbury, England, 16, 49, to south bank of Rappahannock River, in Gloucester Co., Va., 50; *William,* to north bank of same river, in Richmond Co., Va., 51; *Joseph Sr.,* from Richmond Co., Va., to Mike's Run of Patterson's Creek, in Hampton Co., Va. (now Mineral Co., W. Va.), where his daughter Lucy's baby, Nancy (mother of Abe Lincoln), was born, 24, 53, 162, and all went to Rolling Fork of Salt River, near mouth of Pottinger's Creek, in Nelson Co., Ky., 53, 162; then *Nancy* to Beechland, Washington Co., Ky., and *Joseph Jr.* (Nancy's uncle) to Elizabethtown, Hardin Co., Ky., 36, 58-59, 68; *Lincoln—Samuel,* from Hingham, Norfolk Co., England, in 1637, to Hingham, Mass., 16, 20; Samuel's son, *Mordecai Sr.,* to Cohasset and thence to North Scituate promontory, 16, 22-23; *Mordecai Jr.,* to Buckhorn Manor near Middletown, N. J., 23-24, and thence to Exeter, Berks Co., Pa., 24, 26; Mordecai Jr.'s son, *"Virginia John,"* to Linville Creek in Shenandoah Valley, Rockingham Co., near Harrisonburg, Va., 24, 30, 33; John's son, *Captain Abraham,* via Wilderness Road to Green River Lick, in Lincoln Co., Ky., south of Logan's Station, and thence to Hughes' Station on Floyd's Creek, in Jefferson Co., Ky., south of Fort Nelson (Louisville), 36-38; Capt. Abraham's widow *Bathsheba,* and family, to near Springfield, in Washington Co., Ky., 36, 42; Abraham's and Bathsheba's son, *Thomas,* to Elizabethtown, in Hardin Co., Ky., 57, 59-60, 68, to Nolin Creek farm near Hodgenville, Ky., 63, 68, to Knob Creek farm on Louisville turnpike, 68, 74, to Pigeon Creek farm, near Gentryville, Spencer Co., Ind., 68, 82-88, to Macon

Index

Co., Ill., on Sangamon River, near Decatur, 68, 127-138, to Coles Co., Ill., near Charleston, 68, 151-153.

Milk sickness: causes death of Nancy Hanks Lincoln's foster parents, 103; causes Nancy's death, 104; brings yearly trouble, distress everywhere, 124-126.

Mill Creek: *See* Creek.

Morris, Rebecca (Flowers): widow; John Lincoln's wife, 30.

Mudd, Mary: wife of Abe's uncle, Mordecai Lincoln, 85.

New Orleans: Jim Gentry, Abe, take flatboat to, 122-124, 129.

New Jersey: Lincolns in, Mordecai Jr., brother Abraham, 24, 23-25.

Nolin Creek: *See* Creek.

Offutt, Denton: produce merchant; promised Abe good pay, 152.

Patterson's Creek: *See* Creek.

Pioneer: Lincoln boy, 3; philosophy of, 21; Daniel Boone, friend of Lincolns, 29; food of, 59, 82, 88, 90; courage of, 91; son of, 119; customs of, 140-142.

Pennsylvania: photos of, 14c; maps of, 24, 36; Lincolns in, Mordecai Jr., brother Abraham; "Virginia John"; Capt. Abraham, 26; Lincolns and Boones in, 29.

Pigeon Creek: *See* Creek.

Pottinger's Creek: *See* Creek.

Progenitor: of Lincoln line, 20; of Hanks line, 49.

Rappahannock: river in eastern Virginia; map, 24; forms northern boundary of Gloucester Co., home of Thomas Hanks; scene of 1676 Indian raids, 50-51; southern boundary of Richmond Co., home of William, John, Joseph Sr. and family, 51-53.

Reading, Pa.: Hananiah Lincoln's childhood home, 24, 43.

Revolutionary War: *See* War.

Riney, Master Zachariah: Abe's first teacher at Knob Creek, 75.

Rockport, Ind.: Spencer Co.; Tom filed land claim at, 68, 82.

Rolling Fork: (of Salt River); site of Joseph Hanks' farm, 68; childhood home of Lucy Hanks' child, Nancy, 53-54.

Salt River, Rolling Fork: in Nelson Co., Ky., 54, 68, 162.

Sangamon: river in Illinois; photo of Lincoln cabin on, 14g; map showing, 68; location of, 127; Lincolns take prairie trail to, reach wooded area of, 128-134; build cabin on, 138; forest glades on, 147; Abe's accident on, 150.

Schools: Abe Lincoln's first, 75; lack of, 91, 126; need of, 92; none of, 113; Abe's at fourteen, 115; Abe's last, 117.

Scituate, Mass.: 16; *see* Bound Brook.

Slavery: church opposed to, 76; trade of, 80-81; Abe Lincoln writes of, reads about ills of, 116. *See* Indiana, Kentucky.

Sparrow, Elizabeth (Hanks): Nancy Hanks Lincoln's aunt and foster mother, weds Thomas Sparrow, 55; takes Nancy to rear, 56; in fall of 1817, moves into Tom Lincoln's half-face camp, 102; death of, 103. *See* Hanks, Elizabeth.

Sparrow, Henry: patriot, neighbor of Joseph Hanks, wins Joe's consent to marry Lucy; happiness of, 55.

Sparrow, Thomas: wed Elizabeth Hanks (sister of Lucy), 55; writes foster child, Nancy Hanks Lincoln; in 1817, comes to Indiana, 101-102; death of, 103.

Speech: Tom Lincoln's, dialect of, 77; Abe learns to make a, 116; Abe's first political, 146.

Springfield, Ky.: in Washington Co. *See* Court House.

Stevens' Creek: location of, 134; near John Hanks' home, settlement of; Tom Lincoln's family, reception of, 137.

Sweeney, William: (Swaney), Abe's last schoolmaster, 117.

Taylor, Jim: runs ferryboat across the Ohio, hires Abe, 121.

Teachers: Riney, Zachariah, and Hazel, Caleb, at Knob Creek, 75; Lincoln, Nancy (Hanks), 75, 92-93; itinerant, 92; Lincoln, Tom, woodcraft, 77-78, use of axe, 89, history, 93-95, parents, character, 96; Crawford, Andrew, at Pigeon Creek, 97; Dorsey, Azel, 115; Sweeney (Swaney), William, 117.

Index

Transportation: canoe, 82; ferryboat, 87, 121, 129; flatboat, 122; horses, 85-87, 109; oxen, 127; raft, 82; wagon, 82, 111, 127, 133.

Turnham, David: (Sheriff), Abe borrows *Indiana Statutes* of, 118.

Vance, David: holds lien against Tom Lincoln, 72-73.

Virginia: photo of, 14c; maps of, 24, 36; *Hanks* in, Thomas, William, John, Joseph Sr. and family, 49-52; *Lincolns* in, "Virginia John," Jacob, Capt. Abraham and family, 33-36.

Walters, Peggy: 22-yr.-old mother; granny (mid-wife), 69.

Warnick, William: (sheriff of Macon Co., Ill.); Abe split rails for, 145; Abe reads *Illinois Statutes,* as guest of; Abe's frost-bitten feet treated by wife of, 150.

War, Revolutionary: Mary (Robeson) Lincoln's sons, services of, 25; Hananiah Lincoln, others, including Blackburns, Crowders, Hanks, Lincolns (335, in all), Rankins and Wears, 32, 44; Bennington, Brandywine, Saratoga, battles of, 44, 45; aid of France in, 45.

Wear, John: and Jacob Lincoln (Capt. Abraham Lincoln's brother), fought together with colonists at Yorktown, 44, 160.

Wilderness Road: chief route of migrations to Kentucky, 36.

Woodbridge, Sarah: wife of William Hanks, mother of John (who was father of Joseph Sr., who was father of Lucy, who was mother of Nancy, who was mother of Abe Lincoln), 51.